Global Rebalancing
A Roadmap for Economic Recovery

EDITORS
Hamid Faruqee and Krishna Srinivasan

INTERNATIONAL MONETARY FUND

© 2013 International Monetary Fund

Cataloging-in-Publication
Joint Bank-Fund Library

Global rebalancing : a roadmap for economic recovery/ editors, Hamid
   Faruqee and Krishna Srinivasan. — Washington, D.C. : International
   Monetary Fund, 2013.
      ix, 159 p. : ill. ; cm.

   Includes bibliographical references and index.

1. Economic policy.   2. Economic development.   3. Financial crises —
   Prevention.   4. Equilibrium (Economics).   5. Balance of trade.   6. Debts,
   External.   I. Faruqee, Hamid.   II. Srinivasan, Krishna, 1965– .
   III. International Monetary Fund.

   HD87.G56 2013
   ISBN: 978-1-47557-366-4 (paper)
         978-1-47557-827-0 (ePub)
         978-1-47559-164-4 (Mobipocket)
         978-1-47554-877-8 (PDF)

Please send orders to:
International Monetary Fund, Publication Services
P.O. Box 92780, Washington, D.C. 20090, U.S.A.
Tel.: (202) 623-7430 Fax: (202) 623-7201
E-mail: publications@imf.org
Internet: www.elibrary.imf.org
www.imfbookstore.org

Contents

Foreword

In the wake of the financial crisis and global economic downturn, key policy priorities of the major economies have included strengthening the still-sluggish recovery while avoiding a return of the debilitating factors—evidenced previously in record global payments imbalances—that hastened the crisis. At the same time, policymakers agreed that this effort would be enhanced by maintaining and extending the unprecedented multilateral cooperation—spurred by the Group of Twenty (G20)—that helped end the downturn in 2009 and lay the foundation for the current recovery and expansion.

At their 2009 Pittsburgh Summit, G20 leaders gave specific form to their intentions by creating the Framework for Strong, Sustainable and Balanced Growth to be implemented through a Mutual Assessment Process (MAP) directed by the newly formed Framework Working Group led by the G20. At the 2010 Toronto and Seoul Summits, the G20 endorsed the analytical underpinnings of MAP-led policy cooperation, extending the MAP's mandate to encompass external sustainability. The subsequent summits in Cannes and Los Cabos have endorsed country-specific action plans and the promising new Accountability Framework.

The International Monetary Fund (IMF)—working in close partnership with other international organizations—was asked by the G20 to provide a series of both analytical and practical assessments of key issues related to the MAP. This book reflects one of the IMF's several contributions to the MAP process. Specifically, seven systemic G20 members were identified objectively as having "moderate" or "large" imbalances that warranted in-depth analysis. These case studies are included here, and they indicate that global imbalances have been driven primarily by saving imbalances—too low in advanced deficit economies and too high in emerging surplus economies—reflecting underlying forces (such as demographics), structural weaknesses (such as labor market rigidities), and domestic policy distortions or gaps (such as insufficient financial regulation and oversight).

The analysis presented here also describes a series of mutually consistent, individually tailored corrective steps that would improve prospective economic outcomes for all G20 economies while representing an important step toward the global MAP goal of strong, sustainable, and balanced growth. In every case, these beneficial policy steps are in line with each country's own medium-term reform goals. The IMF's analysis underscores that if these reforms were implemented in a coherent, multilateral context, their positive results would be made more powerful. Hopefully, the IMF analysis that forms the basis for this volume will help to build support for these reforms that, taken together, hold out the promise of stronger growth and enhanced global stability.

John Lipsky
Distinguished Visiting Scholar
Johns Hopkins University School of Advanced International Studies

Acknowledgments

This volume is based on a set of reports produced by staff of the International Monetary Fund's Research Department for the Group of Twenty (G20) and the Mutual Assessment Process (MAP). The project was conducted under the leadership and guidance of Olivier Blanchard, Economic Counsellor and Director of the IMF's Research Department. The bulk of the work was produced by a team from the Multilateral Surveillance Division, headed by Krishna Srinivasan and Hamid Faruqee. The Modeling Division led by Douglas Laxton and Ben Hunt provided critical input with respect to the scenario analysis, while Josh Felman and Jörg Decressin helped support, guide, and shape the policy analysis and assessments as senior reviewers. Strong support from IMF management—especially former First Deputy Managing Director John Lipsky—was instrumental for this year-long effort by IMF staff, which was carried out in collaboration with other international organizations, notably the Organization for Economic Cooperation and Development. As a principal interlocutor with the G20, Reza Moghadam—former Director of the Strategy, Policy, and Review Department—provided strong support.

The editors thank the contributing authors—Olivier Blanchard, Mitali Das, Joong Shik Kang, Vladimir Klyuev, Gian Maria Milesi-Ferretti, Shaun Roache, and Emil Stavrev. They would also like to thank Anne Lalramnghakhleli Moses, Eric Bang, David Reischfeld, and Min Song for their excellent technical support in producing this volume. David Einhorn edited the manuscript, and Joanne Johnson of the Communications Department coordinated the production of the publication.

The papers have benefited from comments from external participants at the IMF conference on "Analyzing (External) Imbalances" held in Washington on February 2, 2012. Finally, this book has benefited from spirited discussions within the G20 Framework Working Group, co-chaired by Paul Rochon (Canada) and Kaushik Basu (India), as part of the MAP, which provided the impetus for this work.

PART I

A Framework for Rebalancing and Recovery

CHAPTER 1

The Global Crisis and Imbalances

Hamid Faruqee and Krishna Srinivasan[1]

In the wake of the financial crisis, policymakers around the world renewed their focus on key imbalances in major economies with an eye toward reducing vulnerabilities that led to market upheaval and global recession. Two questions have received particular attention. First, were the main global fault lines responsible for the crisis rooted in global imbalances? The answer is not as straightforward as many presume if one carefully distinguishes between symptom and cause. Second, is global rebalancing essential for securing a durable recovery? A consensus among policymakers has been building that such a multilateral undertaking would benefit the global economy going forward and should be encouraged through policy collaboration.

At the Group of Twenty (G20) Summit in Pittsburgh in 2009, leaders committed to achieving strong, sustainable, and balanced growth. Toward this end, a new framework was created that has evolved over time to support these objectives. An embodiment of that collective commitment in Pittsburgh was the launch of the Mutual Assessment Process (MAP) to evaluate the consistency of G20 policies and frameworks with members' shared growth objectives. Since then, the framework has been augmented to enhance its effectiveness. At the 2010 G20 Summit in Seoul, for example, leaders committed to enhancing the MAP to promote external sustainability. It was agreed that "persistently large external imbalances, assessed against indicative guidelines . . . warrant an assessment of their nature and the root causes of impediments to adjustment as part of the Mutual Assessment Process . . ."[2]

More to the point, it was clear at the Pittsburgh Summit that resolving the financial crisis, sustaining a durable recovery, and anchoring strong, sustainable, and balanced growth required two "rebalancing acts." One is internal, involving a hand-off from public-demand-led to private-demand-led growth; the other is external, involving rebalancing demand in countries with large current account deficits toward external demand, and rebalancing demand in countries with large current account surpluses toward internal demand.

---

[1]Hamid Faruqee is Division Chief of the Multilateral Surveillance Division in the IMF Research Department, and Krishna Srinivasan is an Assistant Director in the IMF European Department.
[2]See Faruqee and Srinivasan (2012) for a discussion of the G20 MAP and broader lessons for international policy coordination.

Figure 1.1 Current Account Balances, 2000–09 and 2010–15 *(Percent of world GDP)*

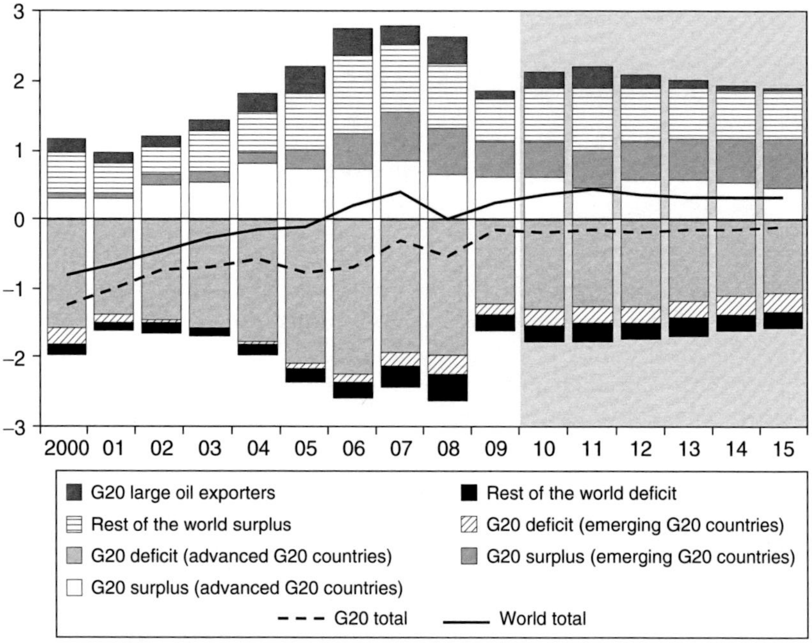

Sources: G20 authorities; and IMF staff estimates.
Note: Figures for 2000–09 reflect data from the IMF, *World Economic Outlook* (WEO). Figures for 2010–15 are G20 authorities' estimates and projections for G20 countries and WEO projections for the rest of the world.

These dual rebalancing acts, however, have largely been stuck in midstream, and as a consequence global activity remains weak, while financial stability risks have risen sharply. With regard to internal rebalancing, while fiscal consolidation has gained significant momentum across many G20 economies, private demand has not picked up the slack, owing both to unresolved crisis-related fragilities and a barrage of new shocks, notably major financial turmoil in the euro area. As a result, growth has slowed, contributing to a strengthening of adverse feedback loops between the real economy, public sector balance sheets, and the financial sector, posing risks to financial stability. At the same time, external rebalancing has stalled, as domestic demand in key surplus countries has not accelerated sufficiently because underlying impediments remain unaddressed (Figure 1.1).

To make progress on the commitments of members to promote external sustainability in pursuit of their broader goals, the G20 asked the IMF to provide a series of assessments of key imbalances for an enhanced MAP.[3] Specifically, the

---

[3]IMF staff work on the set of MAP reports was undertaken in close partnership with the Organization for Economic Cooperation and Development, World Bank, International Labor Organization, and United Nations Conference on Trade and Development.

IMF was asked to undertake an in-depth assessment across key G20 economies of the nature of large imbalances, their root causes, and impediments to adjustment that may undermine growth. Box 1.1 describes the G20 indicative guidelines and how they were used to identify the specific G20 members selected for these studies. The first step of an integrated two-step process—based on G20 indicative

BOX 1.1

G20 Indicative Guidelines for Identifying Large Imbalances

To move forward the G20's commitment at its Seoul Summit in 2010 to promote external sustainability, indicative guidelines were developed to help identify persistently large imbalances among members that warranted deeper analysis. This process identified seven members for in-depth assessments (i.e., sustainability reports) using the approach described below.[1]

A set of key indicators were agreed upon by the G20 to evaluate key imbalances. These indicators were (1) public debt and fiscal deficits; (2) private saving and private debt; and (3) the external position (composed of the trade balance and net investment income flows and transfers).

Developing the indicative guidelines consisted of comparing indicators to reference values to determine if deviations were significant based on four different approaches (see Figure 1.1.1). While not policy targets, reference values were derived based on (1) a structural approach using economic frameworks to derive suitable norms; (2) a time-series approach to provide historical trends; (3) a cross-section approach to

Figure 1.1.1 G20 Indicative Guidelines: Comparison of Approaches *(Systemic rule; at market exchange rates)*

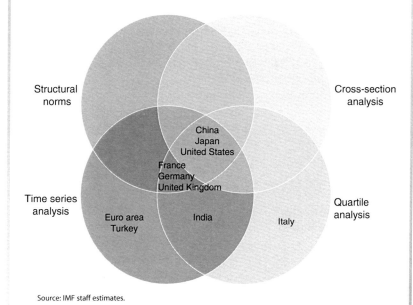

Source: IMF staff estimates.

provide benchmarks based on group averages for countries at similar stages of development; and (4) quartile analysis to provide median values based on the full G20 distribution. Values of the indicators were based on the IMF's *World Economic Outlook* projections for 2013–15.

Members were selected if imbalances significantly exceeded their reference values in at least two of the approaches. "Large" imbalances were identified as such if two or more of the methods found deviations from indicative guidelines to be significant in two of the three sectors (external, fiscal, and private sector). Systemic countries (which account for 5 percent or more of GDP of G20 countries) were evaluated on stricter criteria (requiring only moderate-sized imbalances), recognizing that imbalances in systemic members are more likely to affect others.

On this basis, the member countries selected for sustainability assessments of imbalances were China (high private saving and external surplus); France (high external deficit and public debt); Germany (high public debt and external surplus); India (high private saving and fiscal deficits); Japan (high public debt and private saving); the United States (large fiscal and external deficits); and the United Kingdom (low private saving and high public debt).

---

[1]For a more detailed summary, see the G20 Communiqué issued by the Meeting of Finance Ministers and Central Bank Governors in Washington, April 14–15, 2011. Available at www.g20.utoronto.ca/2011/2011-finance-110415-en.html.

guidelines—identified significant imbalances in seven systemic members: China, France, Germany, India, Japan, the United Kingdom, and the United States. These countries were identified as having "moderate" or "large" imbalances (external or internal) that warranted more in-depth assessment of their root causes, implications for growth, and possible need for corrective action.

This volume is mainly an outgrowth of that 2011 work by IMF staff. The seven case studies provide an assessment of the underlying causes and internal or global risks of key imbalances in these major systemic economies, derived from IMF staff's sustainability reports prepared for the MAP. These studies provide essential analyses and assessments as input for global rebalancing scenarios that the IMF staff envisions would deliver healthier global growth.

POLICY OBJECTIVES

In terms of policy implications, there is agreement in the G20 that securing strong, sustainable, and balanced growth will require reducing excessive imbalances. If large internal or external imbalances persist for an extended period, they could pose systemic problems, including the risk of disruptive adjustments. A central question is what determines whether balances are indeed "excessive" from both domestic and multilateral perspectives. This volume provides a basis to answer this question and to explore the attendant policy requirements.

Conceptually, imbalances are not necessarily "bad." They warrant remedial action only to the extent that they are underpinned by distortions. In particular, imbalances may reflect differences in saving and investment patterns and portfolio choices across countries owing to differences in levels of development, demographic patterns, and other underlying economic fundamentals. In such cases imbalances are not a reason for concern. At the same time, imbalances may also reflect policy distortions, market failures, and externalities at the level of individual economies or at a global level. If so, they are a cause of concern, since they could undermine both the strength and sustainability of growth. In particular, the following typology is useful:

- Imbalances can be *beneficial* if they reflect the optimal allocation of capital across time and space. For instance, to meet its life-cycle needs, a country with an aging population relative to its trading partner may choose to save and run current account surpluses in anticipation of the dissaving that will occur when the workforce shrinks. Similarly, a country with attractive investment opportunities may wish to finance part of its investment through foreign saving, and thus run a current account deficit.

- Imbalances can be *detrimental* if they reflect structural shortcomings, policy distortions, or market failures. For instance, large current account surpluses may reflect high national saving unrelated to the life-cycle needs of a country but instead related to structural shortcomings, such as a lack of social insurance or poor governance of firms that allows them to retain excessive earnings. Similarly, countries could be running large current account deficits because of low private saving owing to asset-price booms that are being fueled or accommodated by policy distortions in the financial system that impede markets from equilibrating.[4] Imbalances could also reflect systemic distortions, reflected, for instance, in the rapid accumulation of reserves by some countries to maintain an undervalued exchange rate.

From a multilateral standpoint, reducing large imbalances is also a pressing need given the current global situation. Large external surpluses in key emerging market economies persist alongside a liquidity trap in major advanced deficit economies (which face rising demands for fiscal consolidation). This configuration underpins low output and deflation risk in the major advanced deficit economies and slower growth for the world more generally. Policy paralysis or incoherence has contributed to greater uncertainty, a loss of confidence, and heightened financial

---

[4]Less clear is what role (if any) global imbalances played *directly* with respect to the crisis. Our sense is that key market and policy failures (e.g., regulatory gaps) in major financial centers (e.g., United States, United Kingdom) were at the heart of the problem. In an environment of strong growth and low interest rates globally, large financial flows across economies appear to have contributed to the buildup of domestic financial vulnerabilities related to unsustainable housing and credit booms in deficit economies. These *gross* flows, which then retreated sharply with the crisis, also help us understand the wider transmission of the crisis in a world that is more financially interconnected. However, this is conceptually distinct from *net* flows associated with external imbalances. While these may have been a danger sign, the underlying causes of the crisis lie elsewhere. See IMF (2009).

market stress—all of which are inimical to prospects for rebalancing demand and for global growth. These issues have come to the fore dramatically in the euro area, where intra-area imbalances, including large external deficits in the periphery, have accompanied a loss in market confidence and a more fundamental reassessment of the Economic and Monetary Union. Thus, understanding large imbalances within and across countries has taken on renewed importance. Policymakers need to move with a greater sense of urgency toward reaching an agreement on policies that will reduce problem imbalances and lay the foundation for restoring the global economy to health.

What this discussion highlights is the need to have a sound conceptual framework for understanding imbalances before determining what policy objectives should be undertaken. Considering both domestic and multilateral perspectives, Chapter 2 elaborates our understanding of how to assess "good" (or normal) versus "bad" (or excessive) current account or "external" imbalances. It then looks at when corrective policy action is warranted—both at the national level (i.e., tackling domestic distortions) and at the international level (i.e., promoting global rebalancing). This framework provides a basis for analysis and assessment of imbalances in the seven major G20 economies in Chapters 3 through 9.[5] These case studies further examine the role of domestic factors underpinning key imbalances and develop policy recommendations to enhance welfare from a national perspective. To conclude, Chapter 10 draws from the country implications of the individual case studies to provide a multilateral perspective on the benefits of global rebalancing and collective action. The multilateral analysis investigates the extent to which pursuit of desirable policies at national levels, taken collectively, can also be complementary at the global level by way of facilitating the rebalancing of demand and supporting global recovery and growth.[6]

REFERENCES

Faruqee, Hamid, and Krishna Srinivasan, 2012, "G20 Mutual Assessment Process—A Perspective from IMF Staff," *Oxford Review of Economic Policy,* Vol. 28, No. 3.
International Monetary Fund (IMF), 2007, "Staff Report on the Multilateral Consultation on Global Imbalances with China, the Euro Area, Japan, Saudi Arabia, and the United States" (June 29). www.imf.org/external/np/pp/2007/eng/062907.pdf.
———, 2009, "Initial Lessons of the Crisis," paper prepared by the IMF Research and Capital Markets, and Strategy, Policy and Review Departments (February 6). www.imf.org/external/np/pp/eng/2009/020609.pdf.

---

[5]Staff analysis and calculations draw heavily on medium-term projections from the IMF's World Economic Outlook database (www.imf.org/external/ns/cs.aspx?id=28).
[6]This approach to coordination—which advocates policies seen to be beneficial both at the national level and globally—figured prominently in the Multilateral Consultations on Global Imbalances in 2006 (IMF, 2007). See Faruqee and Srinivasan (2012) for a comparative discussion of the Multilateral Consultations and the MAP.

CHAPTER 2

(Why) Should Current Account Balances Be Reduced?

Olivier Blanchard and Gian Maria Milesi-Ferretti[1]

This chapter looks to answer two complex questions. First, why might a country want to reduce its current account deficit or surplus? And second, why might the international community ask the country to do even more? These questions were inspired by the G20's request to the IMF to help develop indicative guidelines to help reduce global current account imbalances. Answers to them are needed to inform the design of "rules of the game" that countries should abide by, and to contribute to the development of corresponding indicative guidelines.[2] The chapter first discusses domestic reasons why countries may want to reduce current account deficits and surpluses, and then turns to multilateral considerations for reducing external imbalances before looking at the case for establishing rules of the game.

CURRENT ACCOUNT DEFICITS: POSSIBLY UNWISE AND UNSUSTAINABLE

Why might a country want to reduce its current account deficit? To address that question, let us first examine why deficits can arise for either "bad" or "good" reasons.

Deficits can arise for bad reasons, such as financial regulation failures fueling credit booms, or misbehavior by fiscal authorities that reduces national saving. In these cases, correcting the distortions is generally desirable and will lead to a reduction in the deficit (killing two birds with one stone).[3]

Deficits can also arise for good reasons, such as temporarily low export prices or bright future economic prospects leading to low saving, or a high marginal

---

[1]Olivier Blanchard is Economic Counsellor and Director of the IMF Research Department and Gian Maria Milesi-Ferretti is a Deputy Director in the IMF Western Hemisphere Department.

[2]Given the focus of this chapter, we limit our discussion of the immense literature on imbalances to a few indicative references, without any claim of completeness. For a timeline of global imbalances, an assessment of their prospects, as well as our interpretation of their driving factors, see Blanchard and Milesi-Ferretti (2010).

[3]In principle, removing some distortions in a second-best world does not necessarily improve welfare. In practice, however, we could not find obvious examples where removing distortions leading to excessive current account deficits or surpluses was welfare-decreasing.

product of capital leading to high investment. But even in these cases, there are still two reasons why one should worry about deficits. First, the good reasons may interact with distortions, leading, for example, to dynamic Dutch disease (Caballero and Lorenzoni, 2007). Second, foreign lenders may change their minds, leading to a sudden stop, which will trigger an adjustment that is more painful than borrowers anticipated or took into account (Korinek, 2010).

CURRENT ACCOUNT SURPLUSES: POSSIBLY UNWISE BUT LARGELY SUSTAINABLE

Why might a country want to reduce its current account surplus? Surpluses do not typically suffer from the same stigma as deficits. But they can also arise for "bad" or for "good" reasons.

Surpluses can arise for bad reasons such as the lack of social insurance, driving up private saving; inefficient financial intermediation, leading to low investment; and other distortions. These distortions will typically be reflected in a more depreciated real exchange rate. With domestic distortions, their removal is generally desirable and would reduce the external surplus—again, killing two birds with one stone. Distortions can also arise at the supranational level—for example, in the form of insufficient global liquidity provision, leading to high reserve accumulation. But a discussion of these issues goes beyond the scope of this chapter.[4]

Surpluses can also arise for good reasons, such as an aging population accumulating savings for retirement, or limited investment opportunities at home. And surpluses can arise from externalities, such as positive productivity externalities from a strong tradable sector, leading to an export-led growth strategy characterized by low domestic demand and high exports (although the net benefits of an export-led growth strategy may decrease over time).[5]

Whether they arise for good or bad reasons, individual surpluses, in contrast to deficits, can be sustained for a long time, if not forever. In particular, protracted current account surpluses do not depend on the willingness of foreign investors to finance domestic consumption and investment, and hence are not hostage to changes in investor sentiment. Of course, they naturally and eventually come to an end, as the accumulation of foreign assets increases domestic wealth, increasing demand and reducing the current account surplus. But this is likely to happen gradually, in contrast to sudden stops for current-account-deficit countries.[6]

To summarize, from the point of view of the country itself, imbalances can be "good" (come from desirable intertemporal choices) or "bad" (reflect underlying

---

[4]For a more comprehensive discussion of proposals to reform the international financial system, see Mateos y Lago, Duttagupta, and Goyal (2009).

[5]We discuss the potential multilateral consequences of such a strategy in the next section.

[6]Clearly, surpluses and deficits at the global level add up to zero. The point here is that individual surpluses can go on for a long time, while individual deficits face the risk of changes in investor sentiment.

distortions). When they are bad, a country would clearly be better off eliminating the underlying distortions and thus reducing the imbalance.

However, unless deficits or surpluses have adverse effects, not only for the country itself but for other countries as well, one may well argue that running one or the other ultimately is the country's responsibility. Put starkly, one may argue that every country has the right to be wrong, so long as it does not cause harm to others. To go further and make a case for multilateral surveillance, one must identify these potentially adverse cross-border effects, which is the subject of the next section.

MULTILATERAL CONSIDERATIONS

Three distinct arguments for cross-border effects can be and have indeed been made, one suggesting a case for restrictions on current account deficits, the other two for restrictions on current account surpluses. We discuss them in turn.

Current Account Deficits, Sudden Stops, and Spillover Effects

As discussed earlier, large current account deficits raise the risk of a sudden stop—and experience has shown that these episodes often lead to large financial disruptions. If cross-border resolution processes are poor (and are likely to remain so for some time), then other countries will be affected—all the more so given the extent and complexity of cross-border financial linkages. Indeed, the argument is similar to the one for large financial institutions: large current account deficits—particularly in countries that are large and/or with extensive cross-border financial links—increase systemic risk. Individual countries will typically not take this fully into account, and thus there is a role for prudential measures.

The argument is surely valid. It was indeed central to the precrisis analysis at the IMF of the risks posed by global imbalances. Specifically, this analysis emphasized the high costs that would be associated with a "disorderly adjustment" of imbalances, featuring a rapid and sharp depreciation of the U.S. dollar, balance sheet effects, protectionist pressures, higher interest rates and risk premiums, and output declines (IMF, 2007). Even if the crisis took a very different form, the worries were perfectly justified.

However, the argument suggests that surveillance—and possibly restrictions—should focus on a broader number of indicators than solely the current account balance. For example, cross-border effects are likely to depend not only on net flows, but also on gross flows. They are likely to depend not only on flows, but on stocks, on the level and composition of foreign assets and liabilities, on the distribution of external exposures across sectors, and on the size of the country.[7]

---

[7]In the recent crisis, for example, the evidence points to high precrisis short-term debt as having been particularly costly in terms of output for emerging market economies (Blanchard, Das, and Faruqee, 2010). In a sample that includes both advanced and emerging market economies, the evidence points to large precrisis current account deficits being associated with large output and demand declines (Lane and Milesi-Ferretti, 2010).

Export-Led Growth, Current Account Surpluses, and Unfair Competition

An export-led growth strategy—that is, a policy combination of a depreciated real exchange rate and enforced low domestic demand (through high saving and/or low investment)—is formally equivalent to a combination of tariffs on imports cum subsidies on exports, and low domestic demand to maintain internal balance. This second, equivalent combination is illegal under the World Trade Organization. Should the first one be as well?

One may argue that the first and second combinations potentially differ in their intent. A country that, for whatever reasons (say, poor social insurance, or adverse demographics), has a high saving rate and/or a low investment rate requires a depreciated exchange rate to maintain internal balance. The undervalued exchange rate is then the result of other factors, not of a deliberate policy of undervaluation. In contrast, a country that imposes tariffs and subsidies (and then decreases domestic demand to maintain internal balance) is directly targeting an improvement in competitiveness. But in practice, proving intent or lack thereof may be very difficult.

Can one think of telltale signs? In particular, can the steady accumulation of reserves beyond any reasonable precautionary level be interpreted as intentional undervaluation? Not necessarily, at least in theory. If a country running a large current account surplus also has capital controls on purchases of foreign assets by domestic residents, foreign asset accumulation will take the form of accumulation of reserves by the central bank. The simultaneous removal of capital controls and no further reserve accumulation could result in roughly the same exchange rate, with the private sector accumulating significant net foreign assets. In this case, the source of the depreciated exchange rate is not currency manipulation, but the underlying saving/investment balance.

To summarize, there is a reasonable argument for revisiting whether, from a multilateral viewpoint, countries should be allowed to pursue export-led growth strategies. Even if such a strategy allows them to catch up more quickly, this happens partially at the expense of other countries. As long as these countries were small in economic terms, the issue could be avoided, but this is no longer the case. The practical issue is that, while an export-led growth strategy is likely to show up in a large current account surplus, such a surplus is no proof of a deliberate export-led growth strategy. Proving intent—namely, that surpluses reflect a deliberate strategy designed to gain competitive advantage—is likely to be difficult. Ignoring intent may be politically unacceptable.[8]

---

[8]The complexity of the issue is reflected in Article IV of the IMF's Articles of Agreement, which sets out obligations for members with respect to their exchange rate policies. For the purposes of these obligations, the concept of an "exchange rate policy" is broad and includes domestic policies (e.g., interest rate policies) that are pursued for balance of payments purposes. In some cases, these obligations focus on the *intent* of countries in implementing their exchange rate policies. For example, Article IV, Section 1 (iii) prohibits countries from manipulating exchange rates "in order to gain an unfair competitive advantage over other members." In other cases, Article IV focuses on the *results* of these policies. Thus, the 2007 Surveillance Decision (which sets out guidance to members for the purposes of Article IV)

Current Account Surpluses, the Liquidity Trap, and World Demand

The third argument that has been advanced for cross-border effects is that, when part of the world economy is in a liquidity trap, a larger current account surplus in a given country reduces demand and output in other countries and thus affects them adversely. The argument is logically well founded. It is important, however, to understand its scope and limits.

To do so, it is useful to start with a discussion of the issue in normal times, that is, when interest rates are positive throughout the world. In that case, the argument just does not carry. Countries can run surpluses or deficits without necessarily affecting output in other countries, because interest rates and exchange rates can be adjusted to maintain output at potential in all countries. Indeed, if central banks target stable inflation, the adjustment of interest rates and the implied exchange rate adjustments will take place naturally.

Suppose that a country wants to increase its saving rate. To counteract the decrease in domestic demand and avoid a decline in output, the central bank will reduce the interest rate, leading to exchange rate depreciation and an improvement in the current account. Faced with an exchange rate appreciation and thus a deterioration of their current account, central banks in the rest of the world will then reduce interest rates so as to maintain their output at potential. The global outcome will be a decrease in interest rates across the world, an exchange rate depreciation, and a larger current account surplus of the original country vis-à-vis the rest of the world. Output will remain at potential, both in the original country and in the rest of the world.[9] One may argue, however, that the end result is still a larger current account deficit in the rest of the world and that, as we have seen earlier, large current account deficits can prove dangerous. The argument only goes so far, however. First, even a large surplus in a large country can be offset by small current account deficits across all countries in the rest of the world. Second, and more important empirically, major deficit countries have surely not been "forced" to make the policy and behavioral choices that have resulted in large deficits.[10] Had they not made those choices, both current account surpluses and deficits would have been smaller.

Along related lines, one might also argue that if large "desired" current account surpluses run in many countries lead to low interest rates in other countries, this may in turn encourage risk-taking and lead to financial excesses in those countries. This mechanism plays an important role in some interpretations of the recent financial crisis that see global imbalances as a key causal factor: large

---

provides that members should avoid exchange rate policies that result in "external instability"—for example, in the form of a significantly undervalued or overvalued exchange rate ("fundamentally misaligned").

[9]Appendix 2.1 provides a simple formalization of this argument and of the subsequent arguments presented here.

[10]See, for example, Obstfeld and Rogoff (2010).

surpluses led to low interest rates, which in turn led to excessive risk-taking. This argument again only goes so far. Prudential measures in deficit countries would have been and are the appropriate policy response to domestic financial excesses, rather than reductions in current account balances in surplus countries (Bernanke and others, 2011).

The argument on the negative multilateral repercussions of large desired current account surpluses becomes stronger, however, when interest rates cannot decrease in the rest of the world. When countries are in a liquidity trap—as is arguably the case today in several large advanced economies—the interest rate cannot decrease if desired global saving rises. In this case, large current account surpluses in some countries can lead to low aggregate demand and lower output in other countries. In principle, these countries could use fiscal policy to sustain domestic demand, but under the current circumstances the room for expansionary fiscal policy is severely curtailed by debt sustainability concerns. Thus a decrease in current account surpluses in surplus countries, through a combination of real exchange rate appreciation and higher domestic demand, can lead to higher output in current-account-deficit countries.

Given current circumstances, we see this as a convincing argument for multilateral guidelines on current-account-surplus countries. But it should be clear that the argument is time- and country-specific. It would lose relevance in a world in which the equilibrium interest rate for advanced economies (those for which liquidity trap considerations are currently relevant) became positive—the case that we expect will prevail in the not-too-distant future.

IMPLICATIONS FOR RULES OF THE GAME

The arguments sketched in the previous sections suggest that there are both domestic and multilateral reasons for countries to reduce current account deficits and surpluses under certain circumstances.

We have argued that, in many cases, current account balances reflect underlying domestic distortions. It is then in the interest of the country to remove those distortions and, in the process, reduce imbalances. This part is clear. The more difficult issue is why this should be the subject of multilateral discussions or surveillance. We can think of a few arguments. Domestic obstacles to the adoption of these policies come from several angles, ranging from differences in the assessment of costs and benefits (particularly if the adjustment process can entail short-term costs and long-term benefits) to political economy considerations.[11] One may then think of a multilateral surveillance process as playing two potentially useful roles: first, as a useful discussion of the differences in assessments; and second, and perhaps more relevant, as a potentially useful commitment device for countries to implement some of the required but politically unpalatable fiscal or

[11]We have been struck not only by the importance of differences in objective functions, but also by the relevance of differences of opinion about macroeconomic mechanisms across G20 members in the Mutual Assessment Process.

structural adjustments. (This latter argument is clearly one of the main motivations behind the proposals for multilateral rules for fiscal policy within the euro area and the European Union.)

We have then examined the case in which spillover effects, either from deficits or surpluses, suggest a direct role for multilateral surveillance. We have argued that:

- Worries about cross-border effects of sudden stops justify multilateral surveillance. They also suggest, however, looking beyond the current account deficit to the whole structure of the capital account.
- Worries about unfair competitive advantage may justify restrictions on undervaluation and current account surpluses, but implementation is likely to be difficult. Proving intent may be next to impossible. Ignoring intent may be unfair.
- Worries about global demand are justified if part of the world economy is in a liquidity trap. In that context, smaller current account surpluses in surplus countries might actually benefit growth in the rest of the world. The relevant question, though, is why surplus countries should oblige. One answer is based on a repeated-game argument: a surplus country today may be a deficit country in the future, and thus benefit from such a rule. The argument is not convincing: the world economy is not ergodic, and the likelihood that the roles will be reversed in the future is small. Another, more pragmatic, argument is that in many (but not all) surplus countries domestic and multilateral considerations actually go in the same direction. To the extent that these countries reduce domestic distortions, this will be good for them, and good for the rest of the world. And, even if one could hope for more, this can go a long way toward strengthening the world recovery.

APPENDIX 2.1. CURRENT ACCOUNT SURPLUSES, THE LIQUIDITY TRAP, AND WORLD DEMAND: A SIMPLE MODEL

Consider the following simple two-country macroeconomic model. Demand for domestic output Y in the home country is a function of the real exchange rate e (the price of domestic goods in terms of foreign goods), with an appreciation reducing demand by crowding out net exports, and of the interest rate r, with a lower interest rate associated with higher demand. An analogous condition holds in the foreign country, where instead an appreciation in the home country is associated with higher output.

$$Y = Y(e,r) \qquad Y_e < 0, Y_r < 0$$
$$Y^* = Y^*(e,r^*) \quad Y_e^* > 0, Y_{r^*}^* < 0$$

Iso-output loci for the home and foreign country are represented in Figure A2.1. For the home country, for a given level of output, a decrease in the interest rate (which increases domestic demand) requires an appreciation (which reduces the current account): the domestic iso-output loci are downward sloping. Symmetrically, the foreign iso-output loci are upward sloping.

Assume that policy is used to maintain output at potential in both countries. And assume perfect capital mobility, so domestic and foreign interest rates must be equal:[12]

$$Y = \overline{Y}$$
$$Y^* = \overline{Y}^*$$
$$r = r^*$$

The two corresponding iso-loci are drawn in Figure A2.2, and equilibrium is given by point A. Now consider an increase in desired saving in the foreign country. For a given r^*, maintaining output at potential requires a depreciation from the point of view of the foreign country, which means, given our definition of the exchange rate, an increase in e. The right shift in the foreign iso-output curve implies that the equilibrium is now at B. The exchange rate is higher and the equilibrium interest rate is lower. The increase in saving in the foreign country drives down the world interest rate. In the foreign country, the adverse shift in demand is offset by a lower interest rate and depreciation. Output remains at potential, and the current account improves. In the home country, the effect of the appreciation is offset by the lower interest rate, and output remains at potential. The appreciation leads to a deterioration of the current account.

Now consider the case in which the desired increase in foreign saving occurs when the domestic short-term interest rate is at or close to zero. In Figure A2.3, the initial iso-loci are drawn so the initial equilibrium interest rate is equal to zero.

---

[12]It is straightforward to include a risk premium in the model, driving a wedge between the domestic and foreign interest rates.

Figure A2.1 Equilibrium Exchange Rate and Interest Rate

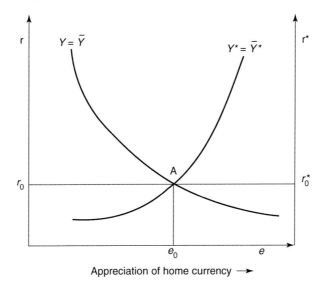

Appreciation of home currency ⟶

Figure A2.2 Impact of an Increase in Desired Foreign Saving

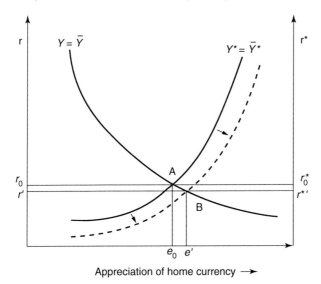

Appreciation of home currency ⟶

In response to an increase in desired saving in the foreign country, the foreign iso-locus shifts to the right. But now that the interest rate can no longer decrease, the new equilibrium is at point C. The home country cannot offset the depreciation through a decrease in the interest rate and thus output is lower. (The iso-locus going through point C corresponds to a lower level of output.) Thus, in this case, higher desired saving in the foreign country leads to a decrease in output in the home country.

Figure A2.3 Increase in Foreign Saving, Zero Bound on Interest Rates

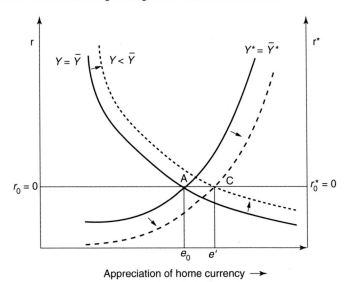

Appreciation of home currency →

This is of course a very stylized model, and one can think of alternative policy instruments—most obviously fiscal policy—that may help sustain domestic demand in the home country. However, this policy strategy may not be viable if there is a need for fiscal policy adjustment to ensure debt sustainability.

REFERENCES

Bernanke, Ben S., Carol Bertaut, Laurie Pounder DeMarco, and Steven Kamin, 2011, "International Capital Flows and the Returns to Safe Assets in the United States, 2003–2007," Federal Reserve Board International Finance Discussion Paper 1014 (Washington: Federal Reserve Board).

Blanchard, Olivier, and Gian Maria Milesi-Ferretti, 2010, "Global Imbalances: In Midstream?" in *Reconstructing the World Economy*, edited by Olivier Blanchard and Il SaKong (Washington: International Monetary Fund).

Blanchard, Olivier, Mitali Das, and Hamid Faruqee, 2010, "The Initial Impact of the Crisis on Emerging Market Countries," *Brookings Papers on Economic Activity*, Spring, pp. 263–307 (Washington: The Brookings Institution).

Caballero, Ricardo, and Guido Lorenzoni, 2007, "Persistent Appreciations and Overshooting: A Normative Analysis," NBER Working Paper No. 13077 (Cambridge, Massachusetts: National Bureau of Economic Research).

International Monetary Fund (IMF), 2007, "Staff Report on the Multilateral Consultation on Global Imbalances with China, the Euro Area, Japan, Saudi Arabia, and the United States" (June 29). www.imf.org/external/np/pp/2007/eng/062907.pdf.

Korinek, Anton, 2010, "Regulating Capital Flows to Emerging Markets: An Externality View" (unpublished; College Park: University of Maryland), May.

Lane, Philip R., and Gian Maria Milesi-Ferretti, 2010, "The Cross-Country Incidence of the Global Crisis," IMF Working Paper 10/171 (Washington: International Monetary Fund).

Mateos y Lago, Isabelle, Rupa Duttagupta, and Rishi Goyal, 2009, "The Debate on the International Monetary System," IMF Staff Position Note 09/26 (Washington: International Monetary Fund).

Obstfeld, Maurice, and Kenneth Rogoff, 2010, "Global Imbalances and the Financial Crisis: Products of Common Causes," in *Asia Economic Policy Conference Volume* (San Francisco: Federal Reserve Bank of San Francisco).

Imbalances in Major Deficit Economies

CHAPTER 3

The United States: Resolving "Twin" Deficits

VLADIMIR KLYUEV[1]

The United States has experienced long periods of external and fiscal imbalances. Fiscal deficits were substantial in the mid-2000s and widened significantly during the financial crisis. External deficits have reflected weak fiscal balances and other factors contributing to low national saving, including external factors that underlie strong foreign demand for U.S. assets. Going forward, large budget deficits and moderate current account deficits are projected to persist, exacerbating U.S. and global vulnerabilities. Policies to restore soundness to public finances include limiting the growth of expenditures (crucially, through entitlement reform) and raising revenues (including through tax reform). Robust financial regulation is equally important to safeguard stability and to prevent excessive credit and leverage that led to the buildup of systemic risk and unsustainably low household saving in the past. Achieving strong, sustainable, and balanced growth would require rebalancing away from a heavy reliance on private consumption (before the crisis), followed by fiscal support (during the crisis), toward an increasing contribution from external demand.

Fiscal and current account deficits have been a persistent feature of the U.S. economy for several decades (Figure 3.1). These "twin deficits" emerged from a near-synchronous deterioration in the budget and external positions in the first half of the 1980s. However, the link has not always been tight—as evident from the experience of the late 1990s. During that time, widening trade deficits were led by business investment and facilitated by large capital inflows in the form of foreign direct investment and equity portfolio investment—both in response to an increase in U.S. productivity growth. Meanwhile, an improving fiscal position benefited from a strong economy, a booming stock market, and tax increases that boosted revenues, as well as from the "peace dividend" marking the end of the Cold War, welfare reform, and strengthened budget discipline.[2]

[1]Vladimir Klyuev is a Senior Economist in the IMF Research Department. This chapter has benefited from guidance from Hamid Faruqee and the support of Eric Bang, David Reichsfeld, and Anne Lalramnghakhleli Moses.

[2]The 1990 Budget Enforcement Act included caps on discretionary spending and PAYGO requirements, which restrained expenditure growth. See Mühleisen and Towe (2004).

Figure 3.1 U.S. Current Account and Fiscal Balance *(Percent of GDP)*

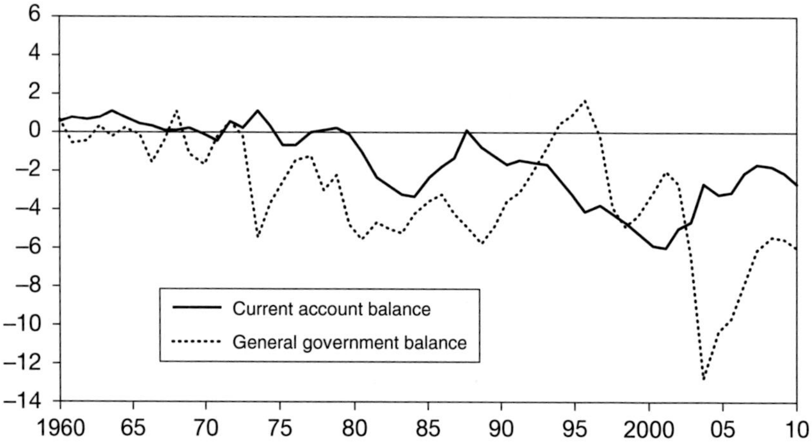

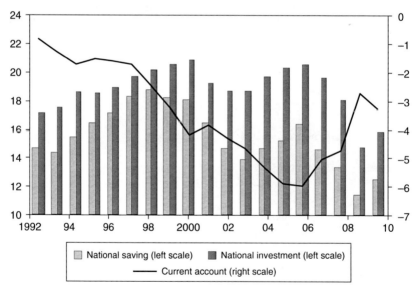

Source: IMF staff calculations.

Figure 3.2 U.S. Saving–Investment Balances *(Percent of GDP)*

Source: IMF staff calculations.

An appreciable widening of U.S. imbalances preceded the Great Recession (Figure 3.2). After 2000, twin deficits reasserted themselves, led by both cyclical and structural factors heading into the financial crisis. Specifically, the period saw the following turn of events:

- *U.S. fiscal balances experienced a substantial turnaround from surplus to deficit.* Fiscal loosening reflected a variety of economic and policy-related factors, including tax stimulus following a downturn, complacency from past budget surpluses, and increased military spending (Box 3.1).

BOX 3.1

U.S. Fiscal Turnaround

The dramatic turnaround in the U.S. fiscal situation from surplus to deficit was caused by a combination of shocks and policies. The burst of the dot-com bubble in 2000 pushed the U.S. economy into a brief recession in the next year, exacerbated by the shock of the September 11 terrorist attacks. The cyclical downturn and capital losses from lower equity prices lowered federal tax receipts by about 1 percent of GDP in FY2001 relative to the previous year. A package of major tax cuts was then legislated in 2001, partially motivated by the need to stimulate the economy.

Fiscal complacency and increased security spending were also important factors. Initially there was a perception that tax rates were too high given projected budget surpluses under unchanged policies, projected elimination of (net) public debt and possible accumulation of public assets, and the political desire to share surpluses with current taxpayers. But even as the federal budget balance swung from +2.4 percent of GDP in 2000 to –3.5 percent in 2003, another major round of tax cuts was passed that year. In addition, counterterrorism measures and military operations triggered by the September 11 attacks added to the fiscal burden. Outlays on national defense doubled between FY2001 and FY2008. The associated turnaround in the U.S. fiscal outlook was reflected in the sharp change in Congressional Budget Office projections occurring between 2001 and 2004 (see Figure 3.1.1).

Figure 3.1.1 Congressional Budget Office Baseline Projections by Vintage *(Percent of GDP)*

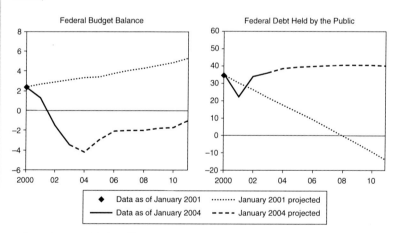

Source: Congressional Budget Office.

Fiscal deficits moderated in the mid-2000s, but budgetary prospects remained worrisome. As the economy came out of recession, the stock market regained momentum, the housing market boomed, and tax receipts recovered some lost ground. However, with an aging population and further escalation of already-high medical costs, expenditures on social security and health care were still projected to rise at an alarming rate. The pressure was exacerbated by a new prescription drug benefit (Medicare Part D) that came into effect in 2006.

- *On the private side, the driver of U.S. external deficits changed from business investment to consumption and construction.* During this period, the current account deficit increasingly reflected falling saving rates and booming homebuilding activity rather than higher business investment following the compression of equity prices and damage to corporate balance sheets. Consumption and residential investment led the recovery and expansion, increasing as a share of GDP. Alongside increased public dissaving, household saving rates fell to historical lows, fueling consumption and housing booms.

- *Relaxed financial conditions, weakening credit standards, rising leverage, and booming asset markets contributed to escalating systemic risk (Figure 3.3).* Easy credit—supported by low interest rates, financial innovation, and lax regulation and supervision—fueled the rapid rise of household consumption. Surging house prices also encouraged a rapid accumulation of private debt and increasing leverage, including through mortgage equity withdrawals. Lending standards deteriorated and credit risks were mispriced owing to market complacency and the "search for yield."

- *U.S. assets were in high demand from international investors, limiting dollar depreciation and allowing large external deficits to persist.* Accumulation of reserves by foreign central banks was a major source of U.S. external financing (Figure 3.4). Robust private demand from abroad for securitized assets added to capital inflows.

Figure 3.3 United States: Home Equity Extraction and Federal Reserve Bank Senior Loan Officer Survey *(In percent)*

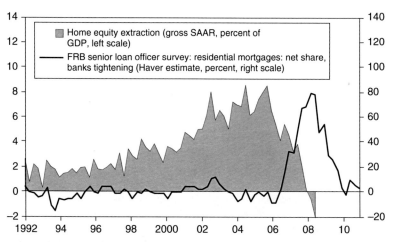

Sources: Bloomberg L.P.; and Haver Analytics.
Note: SAAR = seasonally adjusted annual rate. FRB = Federal Reserve Bank.

Figure 3.4   International Reserves *(In trillions of U.S. dollars)*

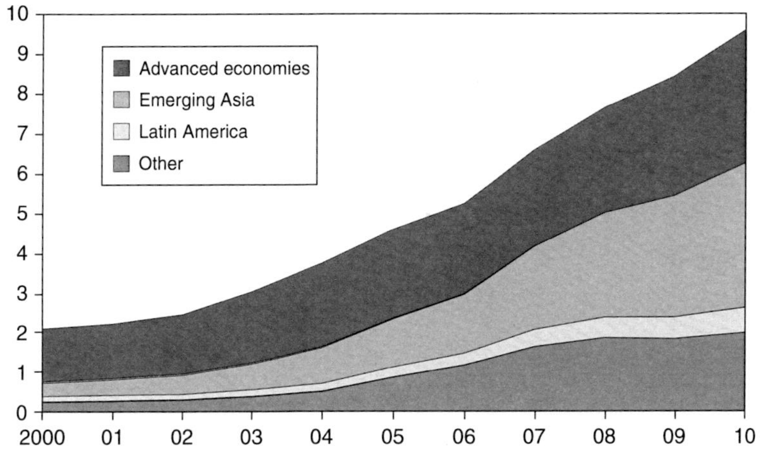

Source: IMF, International Financial Statistics.

- *Some narrowing of imbalances occurred prior to the crisis as conditions began to change, but this proved insufficient.* Mortgage interest rates began climbing in 2005, home prices peaked in 2006, and bank lending standards started tightening at the end of that year, bringing the construction and housing boom to an end. With residential investment sharply down, and given past dollar depreciation, the current account balance bottomed out in 2006 and improved noticeably over the following two years. While the acute phase of the crisis broke out in September 2008 with the collapse of Lehman Brothers, these gradual corrections had started earlier, but unfortunately failed to prevent a systemic financial crisis.

Following the crisis, external imbalances compressed, but fiscal imbalances deteriorated dramatically. The crisis, which ostensibly originated in the U.S. subprime mortgage market, accelerated a narrowing of the trade balance (partly reflecting sharply falling oil prices), despite a temporary rebound in the dollar (the "safe haven" effect), which maintained its status as the dominant reserve currency (Figure 3.5). With consumer spending dampened by extraordinary uncertainty, a sharp drop in asset prices, and tight credit conditions, private saving rebounded while investment contracted. In contrast, government spending was stepped up and public finances deteriorated substantially as a result of the automatic stabilizers, fiscal stimulus, declining asset prices, and large financial system support caused or necessitated by the sharp economic downturn.

Figure 3.5 Foreign Exchange Reserves by Currency *(Percent of allocated reserves)*

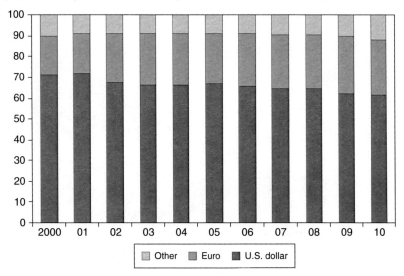

Sources: IMF, Currency Composition of Official Foreign Exchange Reserves database (www.imf.org/external/np/sta/cofer/eng/index.htm); and International Financial Statistics.

ROOT CAUSES OF IMBALANCES

Fiscal Imbalances

Several key factors underpin present and projected large U.S. fiscal deficits. These include (1) structural factors underlying precrisis deficits; (2) legacy effects from the crisis itself on the fiscal accounts; and (3) underfunded entitlement obligations. This section elaborates on each of these areas.

The U.S. fiscal position was structurally unbalanced before the crisis began. Specifically, a structural shortfall in tax revenues relative to augmented spending commitments at the federal level became evident in the early 2000s. The 2001 and 2003 tax cuts reduced federal revenue by over $2.5 trillion over the following 10 years.[3] Although these tax cuts were scheduled to expire, returning to higher marginal rates has turned out to be politically difficult. Separately, after decades of using tax incentives to promote various objectives, the tax code is extremely complex and ridden with inefficiencies.[4] On the spending side, while discretionary nondefense expenditure had been squeezed before the crisis, high military and security spending has persisted since the 9/11 terrorist attacks.

---

[3]Part of that sum includes the impact of alternative minimum tax relief.

[4]The report of the National Commission on Fiscal Responsibility and Reform (2010) identifies $1.1 trillion annually in tax expenditures. For corporations, tax loopholes are responsible for a combination of high statutory rates and relatively low revenue collection. For households, mortgage interest rate deductions to promote home ownership are typically not taken advantage of by low-income households (who need the most help to buy a residence) as they tend not to itemize deductible expenses.

Figure 3.6 Health Care Expenditures versus Life Expectancy, 2007 *(Percent of GDP)*

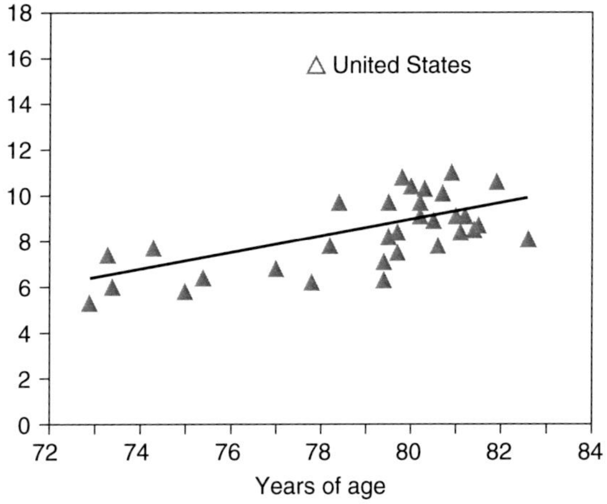

Source: Organization for Economic Cooperation and Development.

The adverse impact of the crisis on budget balances has been large and multifaceted. Perhaps the single largest effect of the crisis on the U.S. fiscal position has come through the revenue side because of output and asset price declines. Moreover, a downward shift in potential output relative to its precrisis trend has lowered revenue-raising capacity in the United States. Direct measures to support a damaged financial system also increased public debt (albeit marginally). Finally, the weak cyclical state of the economy necessitated fiscal stimulus and later made it harder to undertake fiscal tightening in a situation where the scope for further monetary stimulus was very limited. The reliance of local governments on property taxes, coupled with the expectations of a prolonged housing slump, has made their fiscal situation particularly difficult.

Moreover, longer-term fiscal pressures on the U.S. budget continue to grow. Notably, growth in entitlement spending has placed an increasing strain on public finances. A large part of the increase is driven by population aging, which will also have a negative effect on budget revenue and on GDP by reducing the labor supply. The Congressional Budget Office projects federal spending on social security and health care to increase from 10.3 percent of GDP in FY2010 to 13.2 percent in FY2025.[5] Over longer horizons, the rise in entitlement spending will be increasingly driven by what is called "excess cost growth." This means that health care costs per beneficiary (adjusted for changes in the age profile of the population) will grow faster than GDP per capita. Excess cost growth is a common problem in advanced economies, but the level of health care spending in the United States is about twice the average of the Organization for Economic Cooperation and Development countries, and even then with only average health outcomes (Figure 3.6). On the public pension side, social security benefits are

_____

[5]Health care programs include Medicare, Medicaid, CHIP, and health care exchange subsidies. State expenditure on Medicaid will also increase.

already exceeding contributions.[6] In addition, state and local governments will have increasing difficulty in meeting pension and medical care obligations to their retirees. Underfunded private pensions also pose some budgetary risk.[7]

In the face of these budgetary pressures, fiscal rules currently do not impose sufficient discipline. During the run-up to the crisis, the United States did not have a formal anchor on fiscal policy at the federal level. The PAYGO rule has been bypassed frequently.[8] The constraints imposed by the discretionary spending caps (established by the 2011 Budget Control Act) and by the debt ceiling are unrealistically tight and for that reason are expected to be lifted. Indeed this has happened to the debt ceiling on several occasions. While having played a useful role in focusing the political agenda on fiscal issues, these constraints have increased market uncertainty. More credible rules would be preferable.

Finally, political polarization continues to complicate reaching an agreement on a roadmap for budgetary consolidation. The two main political parties' ideological positions have become entrenched in recent years, with staunch opposition on one side to any tax increase or on the other side to any major welfare benefit cut. The political stalemate has precluded a general accord on the contours of decisive medium-term fiscal adjustment. The standoff over raising the federal debt ceiling and the inability to pass FY2011 appropriation bills are recent manifestations. In 2012, concerns came to the fore about the "fiscal cliff"—a large, disruptive, and untargeted budget tightening envisaged under current law—with all major actors agreeing on the need to avoid the contraction, but not on how to achieve it.

External Imbalances

Large external deficits reflected a combination of weak fiscal balances, low private saving, and brisk residential investment. The configuration of private saving–investment imbalances, in turn, was driven by an underlying confluence of domestic and external factors, including strong foreign demand for U.S. assets. Let's take each in turn.

Preeminent *domestic* factors—reflected, inter alia, in large financial imbalances—included key market and policy failures that led to a dangerous buildup of systemic risk.[9] The housing boom and bust, the increase in financial and household debt and leverage, and the decline in household saving can be traced to these underlying factors. More specifically, the imbalances can be attributed to the circumstances outlined below.

---

[6]According to *The 2011 Annual Report of the Board of Trustees of the Federal Old-Age and Survivors Insurance and Federal Disability Insurance Trust Funds*.www.ssa.gov/OACT/TR/2011/tr2011.pdf.

[7]While the federal government is not directly responsible for private pensions, systemic underfunding may create a call on the Pension Benefit Guarantee Corporation (PBGC). In that eventuality, PBGC resources would likely prove insufficient, and there may be pressure on the federal government to step in.

[8]According to the Tax Policy Center, PAYGO, which stands for pay-as-you-go, "is a budget rule requiring that, relative to current law, any tax cuts or entitlement and other mandatory spending increases must be paid for by a tax increase or a cut in mandatory spending."

[9]See IMF (2009) for a discussion.

- *A rapid rise in private consumption, fueled by a housing bubble, was symptomatic of market complacency and an unsustainable credit boom.* This can largely be attributed to excessive financial risk-taking and inadequate regulation alongside accommodative monetary and financial conditions. Overly optimistic expectations about the future growth in income and particularly rising house prices (extrapolating unsustainable trends) further contributed to the decline in private saving and wider external deficits.

- *Misaligned incentives in the financial system were partly responsible for a fundamental breakdown in market discipline and mispricing of risk.*[10] At the center of the crisis was the combination of factors that led private agents to make poor decisions that ultimately created vulnerabilities in a financial system that was increasingly unable to sufficiently regulate itself (Greenspan, 2010). This included excessive leverage and risk-taking in the context of unusually low market volatility, interest rates, and the "search for yield," all against a backdrop of a global saving glut and the Federal Reserve's accommodative monetary stance in the first half of the 2000s that depressed both long- and short-term interest rates;[11] moral hazard problems that eroded market discipline in large, systemically important institutions that were too big to fail; agency and incentive problems surrounding innovative but complex securitization instruments and the "originate-to-distribute" lending model; and insufficient risk and liquidity management by financial institutions that were increasingly reliant on wholesale funding markets that became disrupted when the crisis began (Gorton and Metrick, 2011).

- *Public oversight was insufficient to correct market failures.* A fragmented regulatory system and its frameworks were unable to keep pace with a fast-changing financial landscape. Risky financial activities and credit creation increasingly migrated beyond the traditional banking system—outside a narrow regulatory perimeter that failed to recognize and allowed a buildup of systemic risk in the "shadow banking" system. Even with regulated banks, off-balance-sheet vehicles were used to circumvent existing regulations (e.g., capital standards). An overreliance by investors on credit rating agencies with conflicts of interest proved costly in case of structured instruments

---

[10]See the IMF's *Global Financial Stability Reports* for 2008 and 2009 and IMF (2009) for detailed discussions of such issues as faulty credit ratings; the rise and fall of securitization and incentive problems with the "originate-to-distribute" lending model; the role of mark-to-market accounting and procyclicality in credit; problems with liquidity management; and the role of off-balance-sheet entities and regulatory arbitrage heading into the crisis.

[11]See Adrian and Shin (2010). The role of U.S. monetary policy in the crisis remains controversial. Some have argued that policy rates were too low for too long (e.g., compared to a Taylor rule), contributing to subsequent financial excesses and the housing boom (see Taylor, 2009). Greenspan (2010), however, argues that the main factor was low long-term interest rates given the global saving glut. In his assessment, the stance of monetary policy was broadly appropriate from a macroeconomic standpoint given lower equilibrium (or neutral) rates of interest, with output near potential and inflation near target. However, low interest rates encouraged greater financial leverage and risk-taking in the absence of established macroprudential policy instruments.

(e.g., credit default obligations). Rapid financial innovation encouraged the proliferation of these complex and poorly understood instruments that escaped greater financial oversight. Finally, thinly-capitalized government-sponsored enterprises (enjoying an implicit public guarantee) were major players in mortgage securitization and created a large contingent liability for the government that was eventually called upon when the housing bubble burst.

Key *external* factors involved high foreign demand for U.S. financial assets (including reserve holdings); dollar pegs in major surplus emerging market economies; and high oil prices. Burgeoning external deficits were financed at low interest rates by growing purchases of U.S. assets by surplus countries with high saving, which slowed dollar depreciation, further encouraging U.S. consumption and imports and affecting export competitiveness through a more appreciated currency than otherwise. Dollar depreciation started in 2002 and continued through 2008 in real effective terms. This did have a delayed effect in narrowing the current account imbalance by the mid-2000s, but its impact on the external position was muted by a run-up in commodity prices. More specifically, the imbalances can be attributed to the circumstances outlined below.

- *The depth, breadth, and innovativeness of U.S. financial markets made them an attractive destination for various classes of investors (Figure 3.7).* The safety and liquidity of the U.S. Treasury bond market reinforced the dollar's role as the leading reserve currency. Agency bonds and mortgage-backed securities provided slightly higher returns with low perceived risk and became popular with both official and private foreign investors. At the same time, the United States was generating an ever-expanding array of innovative and

Figure 3.7 Net Purchases of U.S. Long-Term Securities by Foreigners *(Percent of GDP)*

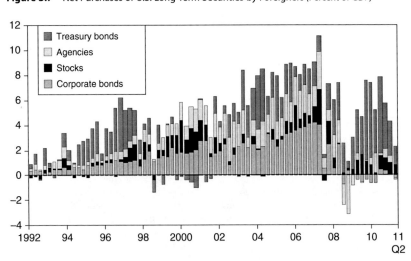

Sources: Global Data Source; Haver Analytics; and IMF staff calculations.

complex securities, which met steady foreign demand. Surprisingly, perhaps, demand for U.S. Treasuries spiked at the height of the crisis (driven by a "flight to safety") despite the fact that U.S. assets associated with subprime mortgages were considered to be its epicenter.

- *Dollar pegs in several major emerging market economies limited effective dollar depreciation.* Currency intervention—most notably by China—helped maintain competitive exchange rates in those economies, created a major source of demand for U.S. securities,[12] and led to rapid accumulation of reserves.[13] Consequently, demand for dollar-denominated assets remained broadly stable and strong—accounting for about two-thirds of rapidly increasing global reserves since 2000—despite large U.S. external deficits that made dollars more available abroad (Mateos y Lago, Duttagupta, and Goyal, 2009).

- *High oil prices impeded a greater narrowing of U.S. current account imbalances.* The United States is the world's largest consumer of petroleum products, and it relies on oil imports to satisfy more than half of its needs. Petroleum trade deficits have accounted for over 40 percent of the U.S. merchandise trade deficit since late 2007. In the years immediately preceding the crisis, rising oil prices offset the improvement in the nonpetroleum trade balance. Subsequently, the oil balance has largely been driven by price fluctuations, although in real terms it has stayed on an improving trajectory—thanks, in part, to growing production. At the same time, relatively low energy taxes continue to encourage domestic consumption.

ARE U.S. IMBALANCES A PROBLEM?

Concerns pertaining to the sustainability of U.S. public debt remain to be addressed. The downgrade of U.S. debt by S&P in 2011 was a clear sign of market concerns pertaining to its sustainability. Moreover, political polarization has cast doubts on the likelihood of a future comprehensive agreement on the path for adjustment. While interest rates on U.S. Treasuries remain at historical lows, they are likely to rise over time as debt accumulates and the economy recovers, crowding out private investment and worsening the debt dynamics (Figure 3.8). From a crowding-out perspective, each percentage point increase in the debt-to-GDP ratio is estimated to raise long-term interest rates by 3 to 4 basis points (all else being equal) (Balducci and Kumar, 2010; Laubach, 2009). High public indebtedness also creates vulnerability to future shocks by reducing available fiscal space. It will eventually require higher primary balances—and higher (distortionary) taxes—to service the debt. This underscores the urgent need for clear, credible, and realistic medium-term consolidation plans or a roadmap to restore soundness to public finances.

---

[12]Demand was primarily for Treasury and agency bonds, but in later years holdings were diversified into riskier investments, particularly via sovereign wealth funds.
[13]Moreover, the growing share of low-cost producers in U.S. imports partially offset dollar appreciation against individual currencies. See Thomas, Marquez, and Fahle (2008).

Figure 3.8 United States: Path of Public Indebtedness, 2001–16 *(Percent of fiscal year GDP)*

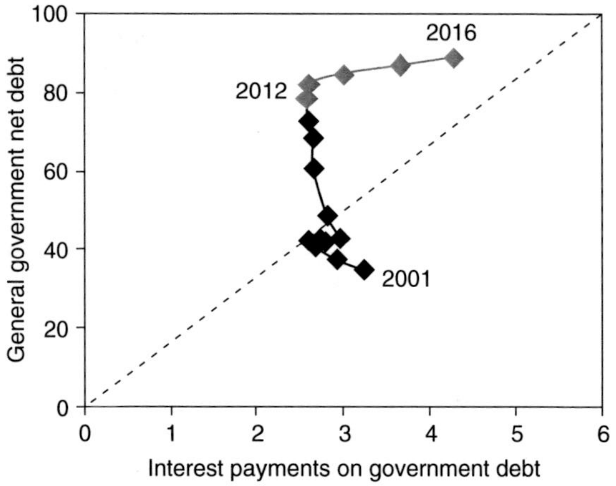

Source: IMF staff estimates.
Note: Projections are in gray.

The United States also has to contend with rising external debt. Increasing external indebtedness may carry attendant vulnerabilities, with possible confidence effects for the dollar. The stock of U.S. net external liabilities is relatively modest at around 27 percent of GDP and has not increased in line with large net external borrowing given valuation effects and other factors (e.g., some overstatement of U.S. net capital inflows). Moreover, return differentials on foreign assets versus liabilities remain favorable from a U.S. perspective. However, there are risks that such favorable return differentials may not continue indefinitely (particularly in light of unfavorable public debt dynamics). Moreover, the willingness of foreign investors to continue financing (at prevailing terms) current account deficits—which are projected to exceed somewhat model-based benchmarks over the medium term—becomes increasingly critical as the stock of external indebtedness increases. Even absent an abrupt adjustment, a continuous deterioration in the U.S. net external position that would result from projected current account deficits would imply growing payments overseas and hence the need for a substantial turnaround in the trade balance down the road to stabilize net external debt.

Should the lessons from the crisis be forgotten or ignored, a return to low household saving and releveraging (particularly in the financial sector) may combine with a precarious fiscal situation to give rise to new financial stability risks. To the extent that U.S. imbalances partly reflected low saving and high credit as well as high leverage before the crisis, there needs to be a coordinated effort to reduce fiscal, financial, and external imbalances and their associated vulnerabilities.

Given the central role of the United States in global trade and finance, U.S. concerns echo in the international arena. An unsustainable fiscal situation, for example, creates multiple problems. As the economy continues to recover, high and increasing public debt would imply not only higher U.S. interest rates but also higher global interest rates, affecting investment and growth.[14] In addition, a downgrade or credit event in U.S. sovereign debt markets or loss of investor confidence (tail risks stemming from the absence of a credible medium-term consolidation plan) could have global repercussions for other sovereign and corporate rates.

Fiscal and external risks are also interrelated. Concerns about the sustainability of U.S. public finances could undermine confidence in the dollar. Moreover, U.S. net external liabilities and current account deficits are sizable as a proportion of world GDP and must rely on significant foreign demand for U.S. assets to be financed. Should demand dwindle in anticipation of subpar returns (e.g., because of dollar depreciation), a mutually reinforcing spiral of capital outflows and asset price declines may ensue. Given the substantial role of the United States in global trade and finance, this possible upheaval would have severe reverberations worldwide.

Financial stability in the United States is vital for the world economy. In the crisis, major risks associated with U.S. imbalances came through financial markets (rather than exchange rates). U.S. external deficits signaled low domestic saving, high leverage, a buildup of underlying financial vulnerabilities, and systemic risk that materialized with the crisis. As seen, U.S. financial instability can have large adverse cross-border spillovers (IMF, 2011).

HOW TO ADDRESS IMBALANCES

The importance of credible fiscal adjustment is universally recognized, but the menu of policy options is wide. What is needed is a credible U.S. fiscal roadmap that combines spending cuts and revenue increases and is supported by fiscal rules to return public finances onto a sustainable trajectory. Broad elements of necessary U.S. domestic policy actions include the following:

- *Rapid agreement on a comprehensive and credible medium-term consolidation road map.* It is essential to initiate the process very soon and to make rapid progress to maintain credibility, spread the burden of adjustment more evenly, and avoid downside risks. Building on the agreement on the debt ceiling, bipartisan progress on concrete medium-term deficit reduction plans would also provide critical additional policy flexibility in the short run. With the economy still in a weak cyclical condition and risks to growth tilted to the downside, the pace of adjustment should be measured at the outset, but steady and well-specified over time and underpinned by a coherent medium-term fiscal strategy. In the near term, it is essential to avoid the overly large fiscal contraction envisaged under current law.

---

[14]See IMF (2011), which also discusses the potential global impact of higher U.S. rates in a precrisis versus postcrisis context.

- *Placing entitlements on a sustainable footing in order to contain fiscal deficits.* Parametric changes to social security (e.g., gradually increasing the retirement age in line with longevity gains and reducing future benefits for the well-off) would lead to well-identified savings over time with a minor impact on current demand. Savings that go beyond those advanced by the 2010 reform are needed in the health care system, including through tighter eligibility criteria, greater cost sharing, and trimmed health-related tax expenditures.

- *Revenue-raising measures as part of the consolidation package.* The room for additional revenue exists, given its low level at present relative to most advanced economies and U.S. history. In particular, with discretionary nonsecurity spending already compressed and only gradual entitlement reform possible, raising tax revenue (including by broadening the base and simplifying the tax code) is needed. Possible measures include further gradual cuts in income tax exemptions and deductions, higher marginal personal income tax rates, a national value-added tax or sales tax, and carbon taxes.

- *Stronger budgetary rules to anchor the process and instill discipline.* The fiscal framework should include explicit congressional endorsement of the main medium-term fiscal objectives. A "failsafe" mechanism for the debt ratio along the lines suggested by President Barack Obama could, if robustly formulated, protect against deficit overruns and other contingencies. It would also be helpful to prepare the administration's budgets using more realistic economic assumptions.

- *Policies leading to stronger growth that would improve the fiscal situation as well.* These actions include further progress in resolving the foreclosure problem, which hangs over the banking system and also gets in the way of labor market adjustment; and active labor market policies, including retraining to facilitate sectoral and geographic relocation of displaced workers.

Active labor market policies could also help reduce stubbornly high unemployment in the United States. Certain targeted policies in this regard (mindful of budget costs) would support labor in problem areas—for example, by facilitating hires of the long-term unemployed (given their very high share in total unemployment) and helping reduce youth unemployment (given underlying problems with job prospects facing this group). This could reduce risks that accompany high structural unemployment with a long duration.

Financial sector policies will need to better safeguard financial stability while remaining supportive of economic growth. Future actions will partly depend on the effectiveness going forward of recent reforms.[15] Financial regulation and

---

[15]In July 2010, U.S. authorities introduced the *Wall Street Reform and Consumer Protection Act* (known as the "Dodd-Frank" Act). The objective of this legislation was to restructure the financial regulatory system to address key fault lines in order to create a sounder and more resilient system. While strong implementation of the Dodd-Frank Act is needed, its effectiveness will only be known over time.

supervision should be adequately funded and sufficiently strong to prevent another run-up in credit (although not so tight as to stifle lending and growth).[16] Regulatory perimeters need to be sufficiently broad to avoid key gaps, head off possible migration of systemic risk, and keep pace with a changing financial landscape. Actions to improve the resiliency of term funding markets that were severely disrupted may also require greater attention. Coordinated global changes in financial market regulation would make it easier to establish comprehensive global safety nets and appropriately tight and consistent credit standards. The Federal Reserve should also be vigilant in maintaining appropriate interest rates and liquidity conditions. Developing the macroprudential toolkit would help monetary policy in meeting the distinct objectives of price stability and financial stability.

TOWARD GLOBAL ACTION

The policy priorities described above inform key U.S. contributions to collective action to rebalance the global economy and support global growth. The main policy contours for U.S. policymakers to consider as part of a broader package of multilateral action to help rebalance the global economy would contain several key elements.

First, substantial and steady U.S. fiscal consolidation over time is needed to restore the sustainability of public finances while mitigating the short-term impact on growth. A sufficient scale of U.S. fiscal adjustment with "growth-friendly" composition (to the extent possible) would require three essential pillars:

- *Tax reform and higher tax revenues.* To minimize tax distortions and bolster growth, measures might include reducing payroll and capital taxes in favor of higher consumption taxes or a value-added tax; increasing energy taxes; and broadening the tax base to enhance revenue collection (by reducing loopholes and tax expenditures, including mortgage interest deductions).

- *Spending cuts in key areas.* To meet budget priorities, fiscal measures would also include cuts in entitlement spending by increasing the age of retirement and reducing benefits to restore the long-term viability of these programs; further restraining growth in health care expenditures; and making some cuts in discretionary spending (including defense) while preserving or enhancing public investment in critical areas.

- *Enhancing credibility.* Clear and effective public communication by the administration and Congress about concrete fiscal plans to realistically tackle unsustainable items in the budget and establish clear fiscal targets would help align market expectations with the authorities' medium-term fiscal consolidation strategy.

---

[16]For example, rules on loan-to-value and debt-service-to-income ratios to qualify for lowest-rate mortgages should be sufficiently stringent.

Second, improvement in the U.S. current account balance must rest on several pillars that, in turn, must be supported by policy. National saving will need to rise to avoid a reemergence of wider external deficits and financial imbalances. Fiscal consolidation will be a major contributor to smaller external deficits going forward. But maintaining private saving broadly at current levels would help ensure that the effect of lower fiscal deficits on the current account is not offset by deterioration in the private saving–investment balance. To the extent that the increase reflects a decline in net wealth aligned with underlying fundamentals and more realistic income prospects, the rebound in household saving from its precrisis levels is likely to persist, and the recent range of 4 to 6 percent (of disposable income) seems broadly in line with fundamentals, though time will tell. Further adjustment in the dollar along past depreciation trends would facilitate external adjustment and rebalancing.

Third, rebalancing necessarily has a multilateral dimension. Given the need for U.S. fiscal consolidation, a prospective contraction in domestic demand would need to be offset both at home and abroad to maintain solid growth and to avoid a global "demand deficit." In other words, the United States would need to rely more on external demand (given fiscal consolidation), while G20 partners—particularly surplus economies—would need to rely more on internal demand (given weaker demand in the United States) to help achieve strong, sustainable, and balanced growth over the medium term.

Finally, U.S. financial sector reform needs to be advanced to rebuild a more resilient financial system that can support strong economic growth and reduce global risks (IMF, 2010). Fostering an adequate flow of bank credit to support activity, but preventing a return to low saving rates while lowering systemic risk, will require better aligning private market incentives (e.g., tackling the issue of "too-big-to-fail" institutions and agency problems with securitization); ensuring prudent credit provision (e.g., appropriately tight lending standards and capital adequacy); and more carefully monitoring the financial system (e.g., avoiding key gaps in regulation, including enhanced supervision of systemically important financial institutions).[17]

REFERENCES

Adrian, Tobias, and Hyun Song Shin, 2010, "Liquidity and Leverage," *Journal of Financial Intermediation*, Vol. 19, No. 3, pp. 418–37.

Baldacci, Emanuele, and Manmohan S. Kumar, 2010, "Fiscal Deficits, Public Debt, and Sovereign Bond Yields," IMF Working Paper 10/184 (Washington: International Monetary Fund).

Gorton, Gary B., and Andrew Metrick, 2011, "Securitized Banking and the Run on Repo," Yale University International Center for Finance Working Paper 09-14 (New Haven, Connecticut: Yale University).

Greenspan, Alan, 2010, "The Crisis," *Brookings Papers on Economic Activity* (Spring) (Washington: The Brookings Institution).

---

[17]In the IMF's Global Integrated Monetary and Fiscal Model, only limited and stylized simulations of financial sector reform are feasible, based on implications for the supply and price of credit. See Kumhof and others (2010) for details about the model.

International Monetary Fund (IMF), 2009, "Initial Lessons of the Crisis," paper prepared by the IMF Research, Monetary and Capital Markets, and Strategy, Policy, and Review Departments, February 6. www.imf.org/external/np/pp/eng/2009/020609.pdf.

———, 2010, "U.S. Financial System Stability Assessment" (Washington: International Monetary Fund).

———, 2011, "United States—Spillover Report—2011 Article IV Consultation," (Washington: International Monetary Fund).

———, various issues, *Global Financial Stability Report,* April and October 2008, and April and October 2009 (Washington: International Monetary Fund).

Kumhof, Michael, Douglas Laxton, Dirk Muir, and Susanna Mursula, 2010, "The Global Integrated Monetary and Fiscal Model (GIMF)—Theoretical Structure" IMF Working Paper 10/34 (Washington: International Monetary Fund).

Laubach, Thomas, 2009, "New Evidence on the Interest Rate Effects of Budget Deficits and Debt," *Journal of the European Economic Association,* Vol. 7, No. 4, pp. 858–85.

Mateos y Lago, Isabelle, Rupa Duttagupta, and Rishi Goyal, 2009, "The Debate on the International Monetary System," IMF Staff Position Note 09/26 (Washington: International Monetary Fund).

Mühleisen, Martin, and Christopher Towe, editors, 2004, *U.S. Fiscal Policies and Priorities for Long-Run Sustainability,* IMF Occasional Paper 227 (Washington: International Monetary Fund).

Taylor, John B., 2009, *Getting off Track: How Government Action and Intervention Caused, Prolonged, and Worsened the Financial Crisis* (Stanford, California: Hoover Press).

Thomas, Charles P., Jaime Marquez, and Sean Fahle, 2008, "Measuring U.S. International Relative Prices: A WARP View of the World," Federal Reserve Board International Finance Discussion Paper No. 917 (Washington: Board of Governors of the Federal Reserve System).

CHAPTER 4

The United Kingdom: Imbalances and the Financial Sector

SHAUN K. ROACHE[1]

The United Kingdom's key imbalances over the past decade originate in low saving. Growth has been reliant on private and public consumption financed by high domestic and external borrowing. Public finances entered the crisis with little policy space and are now left in a much weakened state. Household saving fell to unsustainably low levels alongside an overheated housing market. Against a backdrop of low interest rates globally, financial sector excesses contributed to a buildup of imbalances and stability risks. Since the financial crisis, repair of both public sector and household balance sheets has been under way, notably through increased saving. Budgetary consolidation efforts will need to be sustained over the medium term and the performance of the new fiscal framework closely monitored. The rebound in household saving needs to be maintained. Securing strong and sustained growth will therefore require a rebalancing of demand toward net exports and investment and away from consumption. Ongoing financial reform is also crucial to safeguard stability—a key priority given the United Kingdom's role as a global financial center.

Leading up to the financial crisis, the United Kingdom enjoyed a sustained period of solid growth, driven largely by consumption (Figure 4.1). GDP growth averaged about 2¾ percent per year between 2000 and 2007, close to the average for the previous two decades. Private consumption growth was higher but also close to its long-run average, at about 3 percent, and it remained the most important contributor to overall growth. Investment remained a modest contributor to growth and net exports were a persistent drag. The most notable difference between the 2000–07 period and the previous period was the pick-up in public consumption growth to around 2½ percent, as fiscal deficits reemerged following a period of net public saving at the end of the 1990s and early 2000s.

Strong domestic demand, partly from robust private consumption and partly from fiscal expansion, led to sustained growth but a deteriorating current account balance. The current account deficit increased in the early 2000s and averaged about 2¼ percent during 2000–07. It subsequently fell during the recession, and

---

[1]Shaun K. Roache is a Senior Economist in the IMF Western Hemisphere Department. This chapter was written with guidance from Hamid Faruqee and the support of Eric Bang, David Reichsfeld, and Anne Lalramnghakhleli Moses.

Figure 4.1 United Kingdom: Contributions to Real GDP Growth *(Percent)*

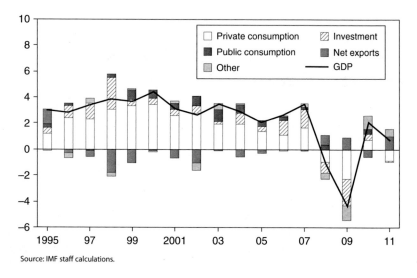

Source: IMF staff calculations.

Figure 4.2 U.K. Saving and Investment *(Percent of GDP)*

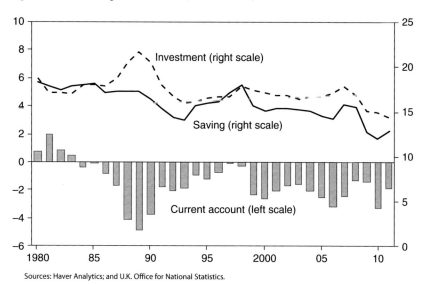

Sources: Haver Analytics; and U.K. Office for National Statistics.

is projected to improve by 1 percentage point of GDP through 2015. The deficit was financed by large capital inflows into U.K.-issued debt, including (as in the United States) securitized residential mortgage instruments.

Similar to the United States, a sharp and sustained decline in national saving explains a rising current account deficit (Figure 4.2). National gross saving was lower by about 1 percent of GDP between 2000 and 2007 compared with the previous decade. Gross investment was largely unchanged, but quite low, over the same period. High external (and domestic) borrowing came against a backdrop of low global interest rates and steady foreign demand for U.K. assets to finance high private and public spending relative to income and revenue. Some of the more specific trends included the following:

- *Household saving gradually declined on a trend basis for almost two decades before rising sharply during the recession (Figure 4.3).* The gross household saving rate (measured as a percent of disposable income) averaged over 9 percent during the 1990s and declined to near zero by 2008 before rebounding by 5 percentage points during 2009–10.

- *Corporate saving increased modestly during the precrisis period (Figure 4.3).* Rising gross operating surpluses, particularly in the financial sector, and lower dividend growth both contributed to rising saving (OECD, 2007). Dividend payouts grew more slowly than profits due in part to higher precautionary saving related to expected contributions to corporate pension funds as a result of new accounting standards for defined benefit schemes introduced in 2001 (Bunn and Trivedi, 2005).

- *Public saving fell toward zero during the early 2000s and has turned significantly negative as a result of the crisis.* During the late 1990s and through 2001, unexpected revenue buoyancy, faster-than-expected growth, and tight expenditure constraints inherited from the previous government helped public saving rise to over 3 percent of GDP. From 2002–07, saving was slightly negative on average as (discretionary) consumption expenditures—particularly nonentitlement National Health Service spending—picked up. Since 2008, public saving has averaged nearly –5 percent of GDP.

Figure 4.3 U.K. Gross Saving by Sector *(Percent of income-based GDP)*

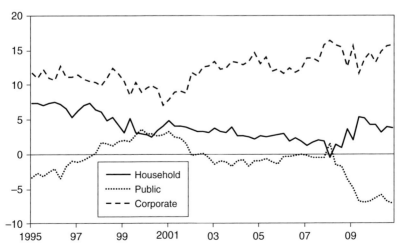

Sources: Haver Analytics; and U.K. Office for National Statistics.

Figure 4.4   G20 Saving and Investment *(Average, percent of GDP)*

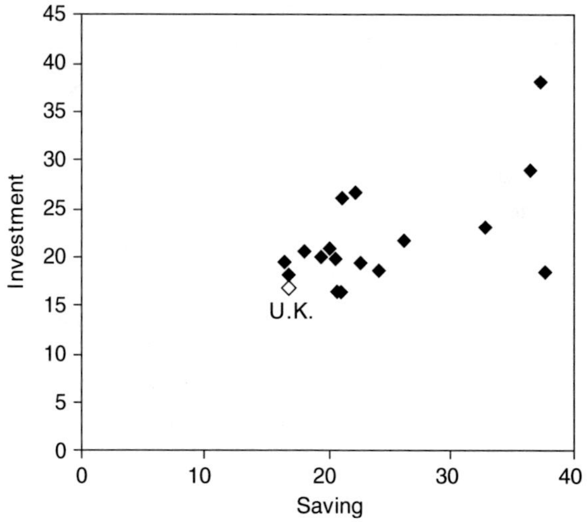

Source: IMF staff calculations.

Investment and productivity are both relatively low in the United Kingdom. The step-increase in corporate saving in the early 2000s did not lead to higher investment (as it might if firms were, say, credit-constrained). Investment has remained at around 17 percent of GDP, toward the bottom end of the range of G20 countries (Figure 4.4). There has also been a persistent gap in productivity levels between the United Kingdom and its major competitors that was only partially closed during the modest pick-up in productivity growth during the precrisis period. Recent analysis indicates that this is due to lower total factor productivity and, particularly relative to France and Germany, lower capital-to-labor ratios that result from weak investment (U.K. Department for Business Innovation and Skills, 2010).

The financial sector played a contributing role in U.K. imbalances, evident in the link between rising household borrowing and consumption. Rising household borrowing helped sustain consumption's strong contribution to growth (Figure 4.5). While the household share of national income fell (by about 5 percentage points between 2000 and 2008, in part reflecting a declining wage share), households reduced their saving and borrowed more to sustain consumption growth (Figure 4.6). Lending available for consumption—related to housing equity withdrawals and new unsecured debt—increased from an average of 2½ percent of household disposable income in the 1990s to about 9 percent between 2002 and 2007. This debt can be used to acquire financial assets, enhance home values, or for consumption. Some portion of this new debt was used to acquire financial assets (or upgrade homes), but as the net acquisition of assets of households remained largely unchanged while consumption rose over the period (as a percent of income), a significant part of this borrowing is likely to have been used for consumer spending.

Figure 4.5 U.K. Household Consumption and Debt *(Percent of disposable income)*

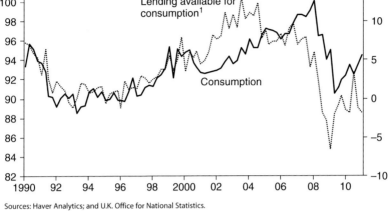

Sources: Haver Analytics; and U.K. Office for National Statistics.
[1]Housing equity withdrawal plus unsecured lending.

Figure 4.6 U.K. Household Income Share *(Percent of gross national income)*

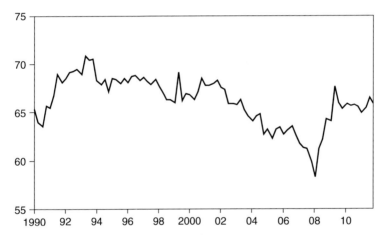

Sources: Haver Analytics; and U.K. Office for National Statistics.

Against the backdrop of low interest rates, household balance sheets correspondingly took on more debt—and became more leveraged—in the run-up to the crisis. Household debt increased by 34 percentage points of GDP between 2000 and 2008. At the same time, net wealth was rising, in large part due to higher house prices, but was still outpaced by debt accumulation. The result was an increase in household leverage—defined as the ratio of total debt to net worth—by 9 percentage points to 23 percent at its peak in 2008 (Figure 4.7). Linked to falling household saving rates and increased borrowing, inflated tax revenues accompanied the run-up in property prices. U.K. house prices

Figure 4.7 U.K. Household Net Wealth and Debt *(Percent of GDP)*

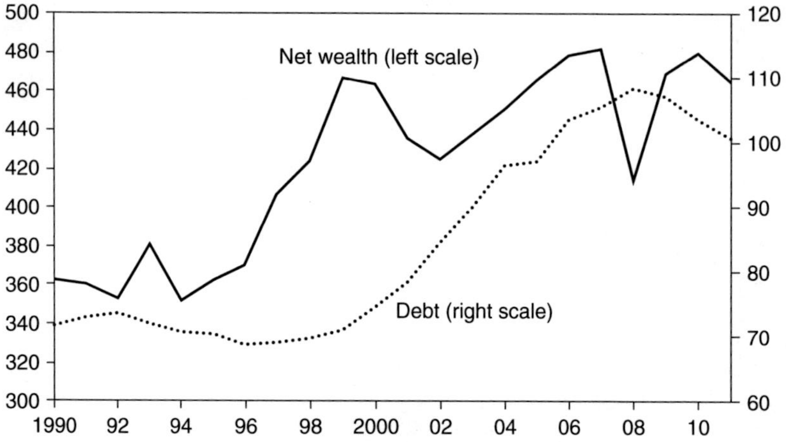

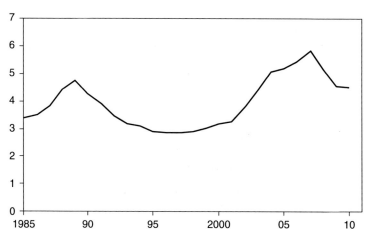

Sources: Haver Analytics; and U.K. Office for National Statistics.

experienced a large and sustained increase (rising by an annualized 8 to 9 percent between 1993 and 2007), well ahead of modest growth in household incomes (Figure 4.8). At the time the market peaked, the ratio of house prices to average household disposable income had risen to historically high levels. Looking back, rising property prices against modest growth in incomes, increased borrowing and indebtedness, and low household saving reinforced one another in the run-up to the crisis. Rising asset prices also boosted public sector accounts.

Following the boom, some of these self-reinforcing dynamics in the private sector worked in reverse. Since 2008, households have begun to repair their

Figure 4.8 U.K. House Price-to-Income Ratio

Sources: Halifax; Haver Analytics; and U.K. Office for National Statistics.
Note: Standardized average house price and average household gross disposable income.

Figure 4.9 U.K. Public Sector Balance and Debt *(Percent of GDP)*

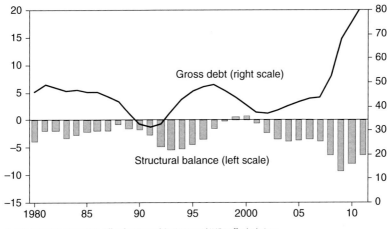

Sources: Haver Analytics; U.K. Office for National Statistics; and IMF staff calculations.

balance sheets by increasing saving to rebuild net wealth damaged by house price declines. Moreover, households have begun reducing debt relative to wealth (i.e., deleveraging), albeit gradually. Notwithstanding recent declines in house prices, housing valuation ratios still remain about 30 percent above their historical averages (IMF, 2012).

Public finances entered the crisis with underlying structural weaknesses and less policy space, before public debt surged when the crisis hit. Public debt increased by about 7 percentage points in the five years leading into the crisis and rose by 32 percentage points of GDP over 2007–10 (Figure 4.9). A number of factors explain the sharp rise in public debt since the onset of the crisis:

- *Much of the deterioration in the fiscal position is structural,* reflecting permanent revenue losses (including those related to asset prices and the financial sector) and a sharp drop in potential GDP during the crisis that, in part, reflects the adverse shock to the financial sector.

- *Discretionary stimulus has contributed relatively little,* in part because the stimulus has been unwound relatively early and rapidly.

- *The direct net costs of public sector interventions in the financial sector are so far small,* although the government continues to face large contingent liabilities.

Higher public saving and less consumption growth over the medium term imply that growth should rely more on investment and exports.[2] Medium-term fiscal consolidation is already under way. Specifically, with public finances on an unsustainable path, the government embarked on an ambitious adjustment plan in 2010 to balance the structural current budget from the 2009/10 deficit of

---

[2]The prospects outlined here draw on the 2011 U.K. Article IV Staff Report (IMF, 2011a).

5½ percent of GDP by the end of a rolling five-year window. Deeper budget-neutral reallocations could further boost public saving and investment and help support growth during the adjustment process.

Similarly, private consumption growth is likely to be restrained as cuts in government transfers slow household income growth and as the need to repair balance sheets keeps the household saving rate high. Tighter fiscal policies and subdued private consumption growth provide the room for monetary policy to remain accommodative for some time (consistent with meeting the inflation target).

The outlook for private investment is brighter, reflecting the likelihood of interest rates remaining low, very high corporate cash surpluses, and relatively faster expected growth in the export sector, notwithstanding weakness in euro-area trading partners, which is more capital-intensive. Sterling has depreciated significantly in real effective terms, though net export volumes have yet to pick up significantly. Net exports are already contributing more to growth during this cycle and this should continue. Over the medium term, net exports should benefit from a more depreciated real exchange rate, as the relative demand for nontradables remains low in light of the ongoing fiscal consolidation and private sector deleveraging.

Repair and reform in the financial sector will strongly influence the rebalancing process and growth. Most importantly, the supply of credit is likely to be tighter in the postcrisis period and likely to restrain demand growth and price increases for housing. Accordingly, to rebuild net wealth damaged by lower house prices, households will need to maintain higher saving. The financial sector will also likely contribute less to overall GDP growth than it did over 2000–07 and, given its current relatively high share of the economy—at about 10 percent of GDP—this will depress potential growth and tax revenues for some time.[3]

Fiscal adjustment plans give strong reasons to expect a narrowing of the current account deficit. Fiscal consolidations are associated with current account adjustments because they compress domestic demand directly and allow looser monetary policy, which helps keep the exchange rate competitive. With overall fiscal adjustment of nearly 7 percent of potential GDP planned between 2010 and 2015, the current account deficit is expected to decline by 1 percentage point of GDP through 2015.

ROOT CAUSES OF IMBALANCES

Low Private Saving

At the heart of imbalances in the U.K. economy was unusually low and declining saving by households, particularly between 2000 and 2008, against a backdrop of relaxed financial conditions prior to the crisis. A number of factors help explain

---

[3]See Economic Contribution of U.K. Financial Services 2010, www.thecityU.K.com.

the striking fall in household saving and, separately, the rise in debt. Recent analysis by IMF staff finds a clear link to real interest rates and house prices (IMF, 2011b). Relaxed lending conditions and increased credit availability in the financial sector further encouraged higher borrowing to support consumption relative to subdued growth in incomes. Similar forces were at work in the United States. Some of these developments reflect the natural response of the economy to expanding conditions, but others—notably the high procyclicality of credit supply and overshooting house prices—are due to weaknesses in the financial sector policy framework and market distortions. Specifically, the following factors contributed to low private saving:

- *Low real interest rates.* Short- and long-term interest rates declined over two decades through 2007 against a backdrop of lower global interest rates. This reduced the real return on saving and redistributed income from savers to borrowers. If borrowers have a higher marginal propensity to consume (as is likely), this would contribute to lower aggregate household saving. Low interest rates also allowed and encouraged households to support larger balance sheets (e.g., indebtedness), against expectations of further asset price increases.

- *Credit conditions.* The supply of credit improved significantly early in the 2000s, which allowed credit-constrained households to borrow more (and save less). The spread of household mortgage rates over the Bank of England's policy rate declined from over 100 basis points to less than 50 basis points in the decade through 2007 (Bank of England, 2009). At the housing market peak, there was evidence that credit conditions had become excessively lax, but in retrospect financial sector supervisors and policymakers failed to respond appropriately (see below).[4]

- *Rising asset prices, notably housing.* Sharply higher house prices—partly due to supply constraints in the U.K. housing market—boosted net wealth. For households targeting a specific level of wealth (e.g., to fund retirement) this reduced incentives to save.[5] House price gains also increased collateral values, thereby increasing the amount of secured borrowing that property-owning households could obtain (notably, through mortgage equity withdrawals) and reinforcing borrowing demand. Expectations of further asset price increases may also have contributed to increased borrowing and indebtedness. Higher prices may have had distributional effects and encouraged higher saving by younger households, but this was partly offset in the United Kingdom by increased credit availability.

---

[4]For example, the Financial Services Authority estimates that of total mortgage approvals, 45 percent were not income verified; 35 percent were interest only; and 15 percent were at a loan-to-value ratio of 90 percent or above. See Turner (2009).

[5]The effect of housing wealth on saving is not straightforward theoretically, since higher house prices imply both more wealth and higher implicit housing costs going forward (IMF, 2011b).

- *Constraints on housing supply.* These constraints are likely to have contributed to high and rising prices. The United Kingdom is subject to restrictive planning laws that severely restrain the designation of new building areas. This has lowered the price elasticity of housing supply, which is now very low and has declined in recent decades (Barker, 2003). As a result, the boom in house prices was not accompanied by a construction boom (unlike in the United States, where residential investment also rose sharply prior to the crisis).

High Public Debt

The crisis and recession exposed structural weaknesses in the United Kingdom's fiscal policy framework. In particular, established fiscal rules were not sufficiently strong. The government actually met its own fiscal rules for the 10 years following their adoption in 1998.[6] However in retrospect, these rules and policies did not adequately adjust for the economic cycle. IMF staff estimate that the United Kingdom was running a sizable structural deficit at the same time as the economy's output gap was either closed or positive between 2000 and 2007.[7] The bulk of the deterioration in public finances before the crisis was structural and primarily reflected increases in spending on public services. The rules also failed to build in a sufficient safety margin for uncertainty, which may have been underestimated.

Projections for public finances were also consistently overoptimistic and not subject to formal independent review. The fiscal policy framework in place before the crisis was often criticized because it provided insufficient monitoring, transparency, and accountability. Institutional reforms recently adopted by the government should address these weaknesses. In particular, the government has passed legislation to put the independent Office of Budget Responsibility (OBR) on a permanent footing. The OBR has already established itself as an authoritative voice in the fiscal policy debate, particularly with regard to November 2011 forecasts that led to a change in the government's fiscal tack, notably a slowing of the pace of fiscal consolidation.

Economic growth, estimates of potential growth, and tax revenues became over-reliant on the financial sector and related business services that were taking on more risk. Thin fiscal buffers became more important over time as the U.K. economy and tax revenues grew increasingly reliant on the financial sector for growth. Between 2000 and 2007, the financial and business services sector

---

[6]Specifically, these were the "golden rule," which stated that over the economic cycle, the government will borrow only to invest and not to fund current spending (equivalently, that public saving will be positive, on average, over the cycle); and the "sustainable investment rule," which stated that public sector net debt as a proportion of GDP will be held over the economic cycle at a stable and prudent level.
[7]See 2011 U.K. Article IV Staff Report (IMF, 2011a).

Figure 4.10 U.K. Stamp Duty Receipts *(Percent of central government cash receipts)*

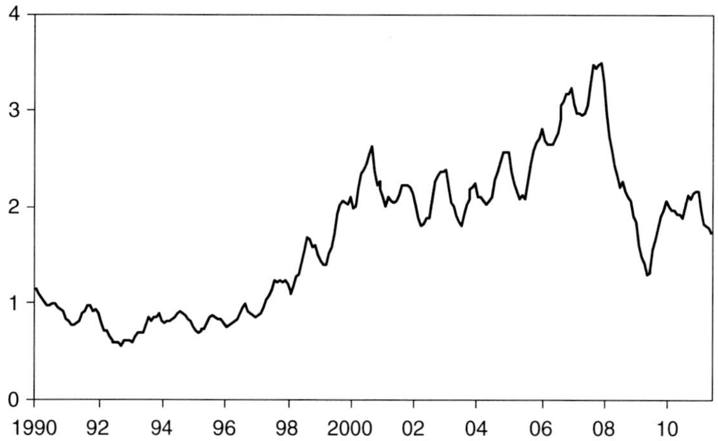

Sources: Haver Analytics; and HM Revenues and Customs.

(including real estate) accounted for just over half of overall GDP growth. To some extent, higher growth contributions reflected greater risk-taking by the financial sector rather than an underlying increase in productivity.[8] In turn, the financial sector is estimated to have contributed about 14 percent of government's total tax receipts in 2007. This tax stream is relatively volatile, as shown by the 21 percent decline in the total collected by the financial sector between the fiscal years 2006/07 and 2009/10 (Figure 4.10).[9]

Finally, revenue was over-reliant on inflated asset prices and windfall gains were not saved. The United Kingdom taxes both capital gains (although not on an individual's main residence) and equity and property market transactions (through stamp duty). Stamp duty on property is progressively graduated based on its value and this amplifies the sensitivity of the duty's receipts to prices. Reports by staff of the Organization for Economic Cooperation and Development have estimated that "excess" revenue related to asset prices at cyclical peaks can lead to the overestimation of structural budget balances of the order of 1½ to 3 percentage points in some countries, including the United Kingdom (Girouard and Price, 2004; Price and Dang, 2011). In turn, revenue windfalls, such as those from stamp duty receipts, were not saved, leaving a shortfall relative to spending when they disappeared as asset markets declined.

---

[8] As noted by Haldane (2010), three related balance-sheet strategies boosted the added value and risk exposure of the U.K. financial sector: increased leverage (on- and off-balance-sheet); an increasing share of assets held at "fair value" as asset prices rose; and writing deep out-of-the-money options.
[9] This includes tax payments collected from firms and income and national insurance payments by sector employees. See the PricewaterhouseCoopers LLP (2008) study of the U.K. financial services sector for the City of London Corporation.

Financial Sector: Lending Practices, Leverage, and Funding

The financial sector contributed significantly to private and public sector imbalances. Banks and other financial institutions aggressively expanded credit, contributing to inflated output growth, asset values, and tax revenues, and eventually creating large public sector contingent liabilities. Households' heightened access to expanding credit, in turn, lowered saving and increased debt. This boom-bust pattern reflected market failures and distortions, as well as shortcomings in policies. Banks were increasingly reliant on short-term funding, including from foreign counterparties, to finance the credit boom. Alongside weaker credit standards, this allowed banks to expand credit much more aggressively than would have been the case if constrained by deposit growth.

Shortcomings with "light touch" regulation and supervision facilitated financial sector excesses. The focus by the Financial Services Authority (FSA) on outcomes rather than business practices and enforcement of rules obscured how risks were rapidly changing as new financial markets and instruments developed. Supervision of liquidity risks was inadequate, as financial firms became increasingly reliant on term funding markets. Cross-border supervision was also insufficient, including the inherent risks in foreign exposures of U.K. banks, particularly to U.S. subprime mortgages. Insufficient monitoring contributed to a buildup of financial sector vulnerabilities that, in turn, contributed to macro imbalances.

ARE U.K. IMBALANCES A PROBLEM?

Large deficits and high public debt reduce policy space and threaten to crowd out private investment—and thus impede rebalancing. The very high fiscal deficits of recent years, if left unaddressed, would have caused debt to balloon to over 100 percent of GDP by 2016 and continue on a steeply rising path to even higher levels. Notwithstanding the likelihood that interest rates will remain low for some time, as activity returns to potential over the medium term interest costs on public debt are likely to rise. This would reduce available fiscal space, although the impact of higher rates on debt servicing would be limited by the relatively long maturity of outstanding U.K. debt. Higher interest rates would also adversely affect investment, which must contribute more to growth in a rebalancing scenario. Higher (distortionary) taxes associated with high public debt may also weigh on growth.

A return to low household saving and high leverage, given large public debt burdens, may give rise again to widening imbalances or financial stability risks. U.K. imbalances are all linked to some degree, and reducing fiscal, financial, and external imbalances and their vulnerabilities will serve to reinforce balanced and sustained growth. If left unchecked, key financial risks—were they again to materialize—could severely disrupt growth.

The United Kingdom plays a central role in global finance and, thus, avoiding large financial imbalances and ensuring stability there is essential for strong, sustainable, and balanced global growth. U.K. external assets and liabilities account for a quarter of world GDP, far greater than the country's share in global trade and output. Global spillovers are therefore limited largely to the financial sector, while trade and other real economy links are modest (IMF, 2011c). Thus, U.K. financial sector stability is a global public good, requiring the highest-quality regulation and supervision. Gradually repairing U.K. fiscal and financial sector balance sheets, and limiting distortions that encouraged previous excesses, should benefit global financial stability and growth.[10]

HOW TO ADDRESS IMBALANCES

Rebalancing in the United Kingdom requires an increase in public saving and greater reliance of demand on investment and net exports. This will require action on several fronts. In the main, fiscal adjustment—supported by monetary accommodation—is needed. This will need to be complemented, however, by stronger policy frameworks and key structural reforms, including in the financial sector, as described below.

Domestic Priorities

A sustainable increase in public saving should be secured by additional structural reforms that address longer-term fiscal imbalances. Higher public saving would increase national saving and lower the external deficit. The pace of fiscal adjustment will, however, need to take account of the dampening effect on growth in the short run. A stronger improvement in net exports would allow for stronger consolidation, which will need to be sustained over the medium term. In particular, further accelerating increases in the state pension age and indexing it to longevity would reduce the fiscal burden of an aging society. Reform of public service pensions (along the lines of the Independent Public Service Pensions Commission) would help improve their structure and better align average public service compensation with private sector equivalents. The new fiscal framework that is anchored by medium-term targets, and enhanced independent oversight would complement these efforts, but its performance should be closely monitored.[11]

Monetary policy should remain accommodative for some time—so long as underlying inflation remains in check. With public finances being consolidated, accommodative monetary policy will help keep real interest rates low and sterling competitive, thereby promoting expansion of investment and net exports. The Bank of England has embarked on a fresh round of monetary and credit easing. In addition to expanding its Quantitative Easing Program in July 2012, bringing the total stock of purchased assets to £375 billion (24 percent of GDP), it also

---

[10]Given the United Kingdom's role in global financial markets, corrective policy actions there to prevent future imbalances and mitigate systemic risk could affect partner countries. Coordinated efforts will thus be needed to ensure the consistency of reforms and to minimize unintended consequences (e.g., arbitrage, location shifts, etc.). See IMF (2011c).

[11]This section draws on the 2011 U.K. Article IV Staff Report (IMF, 2011a), the 2011 U.K. Spillover Report (IMF, 2011c), and the 2011 U.K. Financial Sector Stability Assessment (IMF, 2011d).

announced a "Funding for Lending" scheme in June 2012 to lower borrowing costs by providing banks with multiyear funding. Banks that expand lending faster will receive cheaper funding. However, it is too early to assess the effectiveness of these measures, and additional unconventional measures, such as purchases of private sector bonds, may be necessary if growth continues to stagnate. This said, attendant risks associated with an accommodative policy stance will need to be watched closely.

Housing policy reforms should aim at increasing affordability in order to mitigate excessive house price volatility (affecting household saving and debt). Policies to increase supply should focus on lowering barriers to land access for housing and providing sufficient incentives for local communities to allow development. One aspect of the current system of housing taxation (the council tax) is regressive, encouraging excess demand for housing. It should be modified to better reflect the value of ownership. This would reduce distortions that have contributed in the past to excessive swings in household saving and debt. Reforms would also contribute to improved competitiveness by increasing household (and labor market) mobility and by reducing the cost of living, helping to contain labor costs.

Financial Sector Policies[12]

Ongoing financial sector reform will help support growth and prevent another buildup of imbalances and stability risks. Policies should focus on strengthening bank balance sheets by building capital rather than reducing assets, in order to balance stability and growth considerations. Liquidity buffers have been increased, but the level of capital across the financial sector is not yet at levels that ensure resilience in the face of prospective risks. Enhanced supervision and oversight are needed to prevent imprudent credit lending and excessive leverage that contributed to low saving. It is also essential to address "too-big-to-fail" issues, including by legislating reforms proposed by the Vickers Commission, as described below.

The macroprudential toolkit should be enhanced and actively used. Monetary policy working alone through interest rates may not be sufficient to safeguard both price and financial stability. The newly formed Financial Policy Committee (FPC) should focus on tools that are most effective against the credit cycle—including loan-to-value ratios—and minimize efficiency costs and scope for regulatory arbitrage.

To safeguard stability, continued buildup of capital and liquidity buffers is essential for resilience to shocks. Specifically, the FPC and the FSA should continue to encourage banks to raise external capital as early as is feasible, while linking the approval of dividends and variable remuneration to the outcome of stress tests. In this context, the FPC should also clarify its expectations about the transition path to Basel III capital ratios, as an accelerated pace could exacerbate deleveraging and have adverse cyclical implications.

---

[12]This section draws extensively on the 2012 U.K. Article IV Staff Report (IMF, 2012).

Since the introduction of the new liquidity regime in 2010, liquidity requirements in the United Kingdom have been more stringent than in other jurisdictions. This has proved effective in strengthening banks' liquidity and funding positions, but may have constrained credit availability, particularly as market stress related to the euro area crisis intensified. Going forward, the FPC should evaluate liquidity requirements with a view to converging into the phase-in schedule agreed upon internationally, while taking into account cyclical considerations and the availability of liquidity insurance from the Bank of England. At the same time, banks should be encouraged to continue to improve their funding profiles by expanding their deposit bases and lengthening the term of their wholesale funding. Given U.K. banks' vulnerabilities to funding shocks, the Bank of England should stand ready to provide liquidity through a range of facilities if strains from the euro area crisis intensify. In this regard, banks' prepositioning of collateral facilitates potential access to these liquidity operations.

The United Kingdom is moving toward a permanent legal basis for a new supervisory framework, one important objective of which should be to promote prudent lending. A Financial Services Bill to provide a permanent legal basis for the new framework is currently before Parliament, and is expected to come into force in early 2013. It will create a new Prudential Regulation Authority (PRA)—a subsidiary of the Bank of England—responsible for prudential regulation of banks, large insurance companies, and large investment firms. The FPC will be in charge of macroprudential policy. The result should be greater integration of microprudential and macroprudential supervision to better safeguard financial stability. A separate agency, the Financial Conduct Authority, will be responsible for the conduct and regulation of secondary markets, investment funds, investment firms, and small insurance companies, as well as consumer protection issues across all institutions. Successful navigation of the transition, combined with the new model of intensified supervision, will require skillful management and a serious commitment of resources. To avoid a return to weaker lending standards and mispricing of credit risks that contributed to excessive borrowing and low household saving, the new supervisory framework should:

- *Strengthen the FSA's assessment of bank processes*, including loan classification, determination of impairment, and valuation practices.[13]

- *Introduce a proactive intervention framework.* It is important that framework legislation include explicit support for early intervention by the supervisor in dealing with prudential problems.

- *Provide the regulatory authority with oversight powers at the holding company level.* This will improve consolidated supervision.

---

[13]The FSA is conducting a review of mortgage markets that addresses some of these issues. See FSA (2009).

• *Enhance data reporting standards.* The United Kingdom lags behind many other countries in standards for the public disclosure of bank and insurance sector data. Regular and comparable data on an institutional basis should be published, including nonconfidential data from prudential returns.

Progress in addressing too-important-to-fail issues needs to be further advanced to restrain excessive risk-taking. Specifically, incentives for excessive leverage could be reduced through further tax reform. Ring-fencing of retail operations and the establishment of depositor preference would improve resolvability of the retail entity.[14] However, ring-fencing should be weighed against the costs as it does not necessarily improve resolvability of the whole entity, unless complemented by more comprehensive measures that require international coordination.

TOWARD GLOBAL ACTION

The United Kingdom's contribution to collective action and global rebalancing would rely mainly on longer-term fiscal consolidation. This should not, however, detract from near-term considerations, where policy flexibility will remain important given heightened global uncertainty. In particular, further longer-term reforms to entitlement programs such as the state pension and public service pensions should be implemented beyond 2016. Other measures could include additional reforms to reduce the relatively high share of the working-age population that receives disability benefits. As well as contributing to the fiscal consolidation effort, this would also boost the supply of labor (OECD, 2011).

These measures should have positive domestic growth effects and contribute to global rebalancing over the medium term.

REFERENCES

Bank of England, 2009, *Quarterly Bulletin 2009 Q3*, Vol. 49 No. 3 (London: Bank of England).

Barker, Kate, 2003, "Review of Housing Supply Analysis: Securing our Future Housing Needs," Interim Report (London: HM Treasury).

Bunn, Philip, and Kamakshya Trivedi, 2005, "Corporate Expenditures and Pension Contributions: Evidence from U.K. Company Accounts," Bank of England Working Paper No. 275 (London: Bank of England).

Financial Services Authority (FSA), 2009, "Mortgage Market Review," FSA Discussion Paper 09/3 (London: Financial Services Authority).

Girouard, N., and R. Price, 2004, "Asset Price Cycles, 'One-Off' Factors and Structural Budget Balances," OECD Economics Department Working Paper No. 391 (Paris: Organization for Economic Cooperation and Development).

Haldane, Andrew, 2010, "The Contribution of the Financial Sector Miracle or Mirage?" Speech at the Future of Finance Conference, London, July 14.

---

[14]This would elevate claims of depositors on assets of a failed institution over claims of general creditors.

International Monetary Fund (IMF), 2011a, "United Kingdom: 2011 Article IV Consultation—Staff Report," IMF Country Report No.11/220 (Washington: International Monetary Fund).

———, 2011b, "What Drives the U.K.'s Household Saving Rate," in *United Kingdom: Selected Issues Paper,* IMF Country Report No. 11/221 (Washington: International Monetary Fund).

———, 2011c, "United Kingdom: Spillover Report for the 2011 Article IV Consultation," IMF Country Report No. 11/225 (Washington: International Monetary Fund).

———, 2011d, "United Kingdom: Financial Sector Stability Assessment," IMF Country Report No. 11/222 (Washington: International Monetary Fund).

———, 2012, "United Kingdom: 2012 Article IV Consultation," IMF Country Report No. 12/190 (Washington: International Monetary Fund).

Organization for Economic Cooperation and Development (OECD), 2007, *OECD Economic Outlook,* No. 82, December (Paris: Organization for Economic Cooperation and Development).

———, 2011, *Economic Policy Reforms 2011: Going for Growth* (Paris: Organization for Economic Cooperation and Development).

Price, R., and T. Dang, 2011, "Adjusting Fiscal Balances for Asset Price Cycles," OECD Economics Department Working Paper No. 868 (Paris: Organization for Economic Cooperation and Development).

PricewaterhouseCoopers LLP, 2008, *Total Tax Contribution of UK Financial Services*, Report prepared for the City of London Corporation (December). (London: PricewaterhouseCoopers LLP).

Turner, Adair, 2009, "The Mortgage Market: Issues for Debate," speech at the Financial Services Authority Mortgage Conference, May 12, London. www.fsa.gov.uk/library/communication/speeches/2009/0512_at.shtml

U.K. Department for Business Innovation and Skills, 2010, "Economic Growth," BIS Economic Paper No. 9, November (London: U.K. Department for Business Innovation and Skills).

CHAPTER 5

France: Imbalances and Declining Competitiveness

JOONG SHIK KANG[1]

France's external balances over the past decade have gradually deteriorated from surplus to moderate deficit, reflecting worsening competitiveness on the back of declining trend growth. Rising public debt prior to the crisis—reflecting budgetary pressures from local governments and social security administrations—increased significantly due to crisis-related costs. Going forward, France needs to improve its competitiveness in order to keep external deficits in check and reduce its public debt to ensure fiscal sustainability. A comprehensive strategy to boost growth and productive potential includes strengthening incentives for work as well as competition in product and services markets.

France's current account balance has deteriorated gradually since the late 1990s. The current account went from a surplus of 3.1 percent of GDP in 1999 to a deficit of 2.2 percent in 2011 (Figure 5.1). This was led by a worsening of the trade balance in goods and services, which moved from surplus (2.5 percent of GDP in 1999) to deficit (2.8 percent in 2011). Income and transfer balances have been relatively stable.

The deterioration of the current account during the first half of the 2000s was cyclical, as stronger domestic demand in France relative to its key trading partners, notably Germany, resulted in worsening net exports. However, since the mid-2000s the deterioration has been largely due to a worsening performance of exports, with France's export growth lagging behind its key competitors.

From a saving-investment perspective, the current account deterioration between 1999 and 2007 (by 4.2 percentage points of GDP) was driven largely by a narrowing of the private saving–investment balance on account of higher investment in construction and services (2.8 percentage points of GDP) (Figure 5.2). After 2007, notwithstanding a significant improvement in the private saving–investment balance, the current account deficit widened further as a result of a sizable deterioration of the public sector saving–investment balance (by 3.8 percentage points of GDP by 2010) (Figure 5.3).

[1]Joong Shik Kang is an economist in the IMF Research Department. This chapter was written with guidance from Emil Stavrev and with support from Eric Bang, David Reichsfeld, and Anne Lalramng-hakhleli Moses.

Figure 5.1 France: Current Account Balance Components *(Percent of GDP)*

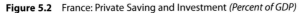

Source: IMF staff calculations.

Figure 5.2 France: Private Saving and Investment *(Percent of GDP)*

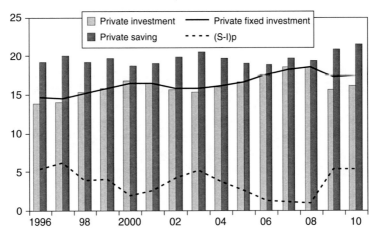

Source: IMF staff calculations.
Note: (S-I)p refers to saving–investment balances in the private sector.

The current account is projected to improve only gradually over the medium term on account of sluggish demand from the rest of Europe and continuing competitiveness issues.

Fiscal balances improved significantly in the run-up to the Economic and Monetary Union (EMU), were generally weak during the EMU, and deteriorated significantly following the recent crisis.[2] To meet the Maastricht criteria, France

---

[2]Fiscal balances include the central government, local governments, and the social security administration.

Figure 5.3 France: Private and Public Saving–Investment Balances *(Percent of GDP)*

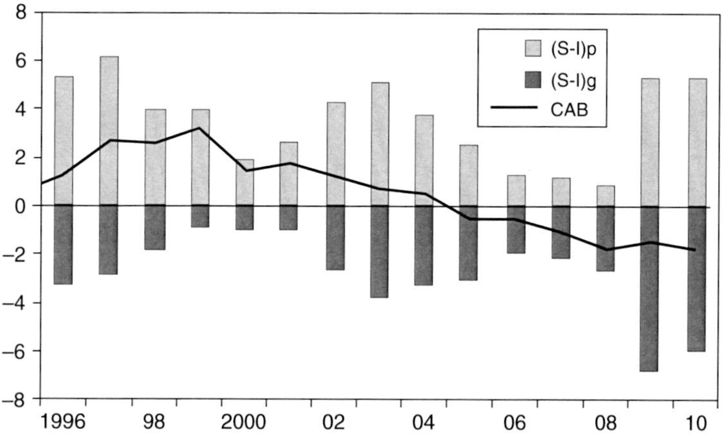

Source: IMF staff calculations.
Note: CAB refers to current account balance; (S–I)p refers to saving–investment balance in the private sector; and (S–I)g refers to the saving–investment balance in the government sector.

introduced a medium-term consolidation plan in 1994. The general government deficit was reduced significantly to 1.5 percent of GDP in 2000 (from over 6 percent in 1993), while public debt declined to about 57 percent as a share of GDP in 2001 after peaking near 60 percent in 1998.

In the early 2000s, rising expenditures by local governments and social security administrations pushed up, through transfers, the general government fiscal deficit. Overruns in social security spending continued in the early 2000s, partly undoing the gains from the previous consolidation. The deficit exceeded 4 percent of GDP by 2003. Under the European Union's rules, France entered the Excessive Deficit Procedures (EDP) of the Stability and Growth Pact (SGP). The significant consolidation package in response to the EDP, helped by the global economic boom, reduced the deficit to below 3 percent of GDP by 2005.

Most recently, public finances deteriorated significantly in the context of the global crisis. Crisis-related costs, including fiscal stimulus, on the back of declining trend growth, resulted in sizable general government deficits (over 7 percent of GDP in 2009–10), while public debt exceeded 80 percent of GDP in 2010 and is projected to increase further in the near term (Figure 5.4). Thus, France entered the EDP again in 2009.

Going forward, fiscal balances are projected to improve. The authorities have committed to ambitious fiscal deficit targets to bring down the deficit significantly (to the SGP target of 3 percent of GDP by 2013 and further to 2.2 percent by 2014) and put the public debt on a declining path as of 2014. The implementation of pension reform enacted in late 2010—which includes a gradual increase of the legal retirement age from 60 to 62 years of age,[3] an increase in the full

---

[3]The new administration elected in 2012 restored the early retirement age of 60 years for workers who began to work before the age of 20.

Figure 5.4 France: General Government Accounts *(Percent of GDP)*

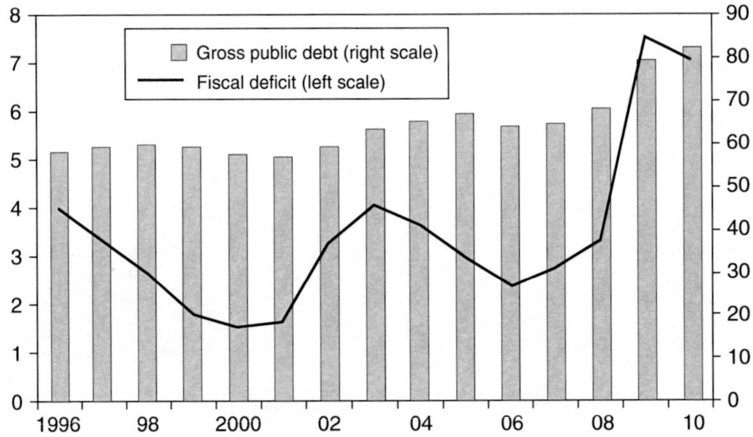

Source: IMF staff calculations.

pension age from 65 to 67, and an extension of the contributory period to 41.5 years for people born after 1955 (to be adjusted in line with gains in life expectancy)—will also help lower the deficits over the long term. These changes will help achieve financial equilibrium in the pension system by 2018 from a current deficit of almost 1.5 percent of GDP.

ROOT CAUSES OF IMBALANCES

Reflecting structural factors and the weakness of fiscal institutions, public finances in France were weak prior to the crisis, despite relatively strong growth, and have since deteriorated significantly owing to crisis-related costs and countercyclical discretionary policies. The external current account gradually deteriorated from a surplus in the early 2000s to a deficit by the end of the decade, driven by strong domestic demand and a loss in competitiveness.

Fiscal Imbalances

The deterioration of French public finances over the past decade reflects structural factors and the costs associated with the global financial crisis. In the context of some weakness in fiscal institutions, the fiscal position worsened in the run-up to the crisis, largely due to rising social security spending. Crisis-related costs have only added to the fiscal burden since.

Specifically, structural factors, including aging-related social security expenditure, have contributed to the gradual deterioration of the fiscal balance. While cyclical factors and corresponding consolidation efforts have accounted for large fluctuations in the fiscal balance, the structural balance has remained weak,

Figure 5.5 France: Fiscal Indicators *(Percent of nominal GDP)*

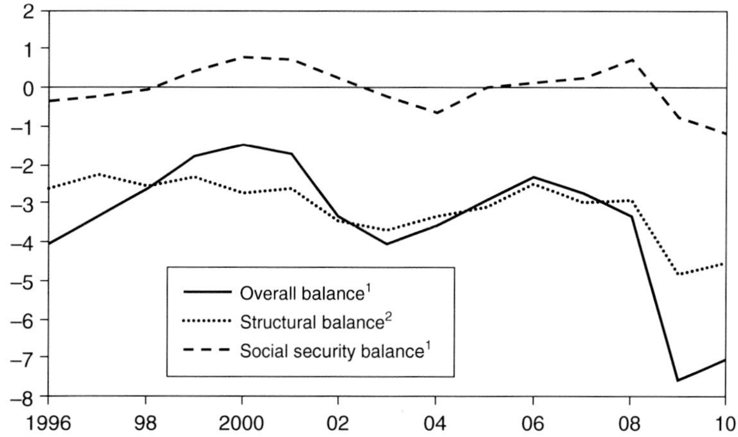

Source: IMF staff calculations.
[1]Maastricht definition. Estimate for 2010 includes one-off transfer to Organismes Divers d'Administration Centrale for future-oriented investments, which amounts to about 0.6 percent of GDP.
[2]In percent of potential GDP.

mainly due to rising social security spending, including on pension and health care. Despite several efforts to increase the efficiency of the pension and health care systems, expenditure overruns on social security have persisted, contributing to the weakening of the fiscal position.

Weaknesses in fiscal institutions have hampered efforts to restore fiscal sustainability. Strong growth in the mid-2000s did not lead to a much-needed fiscal consolidation (Figure 5.5). The significant decentralization efforts in the early 2000s resulted in a rapid growth of local government spending (5 percent annually on average during 2001–10). While the favorable global economic boom contributed to the end of the first EDP in the mid-2000s, the deficit targets set in the country's successive stability programs were frequently missed, mainly due to spending overruns by local governments and the social security system—which accounted for about 21½ percent and 46¼ percent of total expenditures, respectively, as of 2009—but also by the central government in the second half of the 2000s (Figure 5.6).

Finally, public finances deteriorated significantly in the context of the recent crisis, with both the deficit and the debt rising sharply. In addition to the full operation of automatic stabilizers, the government provided discretionary fiscal stimulus in the amount of 2¼ percent of GDP over 2009–10 to cushion the downturn.[4] Combined with declining trend growth, these measures have pushed the general government deficit to above 7 percent of GDP, and public debt has increased to over 80 percent of GDP.

---

[4]Only part of this fiscal stimulus had an impact on the general government deficit, as some measures (e.g., public enterprise investments) are not included in the general government accounts.

Figure 5.6 France: Overruns in Real Spending Growth *(Percent)*

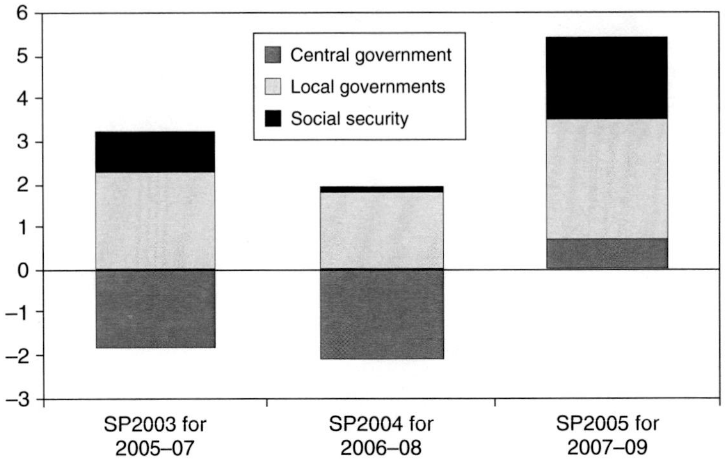

Source: Martin, Tytell, and Yakadina (2011).
Note: SP = Stability Program.

External Imbalances

The current account has deteriorated largely due to the declining competitiveness of French exports as well as strong domestic demand.[5] The deterioration of the trade balance in the early 2000s was mainly due to cyclically lower foreign demand. While France faced consistently lower foreign demand than its large euro-area neighbors, France's strong domestic demand growth—exceeding that of its largest trading partner Germany by 3 percent a year on average over 2001–05—resulted in strong French imports and worsening net exports, which turned negative in 2005 (Figure 5.7).

Since 2005, export growth in France has fallen significantly below the euro-area average, pulling down French export market shares both worldwide and within the euro area (Figure 5.8). Combined with strong domestic demand, trade and current account balances continued to deteriorate, raising concerns about the competitiveness of French exports. The current account deteriorated further during the Great Recession as public sector demand, supported by the stimulus, more than offset the decline of private sector demand.

The deteriorating competitiveness of French exports, and associated loss of market share, reflects both price and nonprice factors. France has lost about 2½ percentage points of world export market share in the last decade.[6] While most advanced economies have lost market share owing to the increasing role of emerging market economies in global trade, France's loss has been more severe than that of

---

[5]Higher energy costs also contributed to the worsening current account during 2005–08.
[6]Export market share is calculated by dividing France's exports by world imports. The European Commission (2010) also pointed out that France's share of exports of goods in world trade (including intra-EU exports) declined by 2.2 percentage points between 1998 and 2008.

Figure 5.7 Domestic Demand Growth *(Annual percent change)*

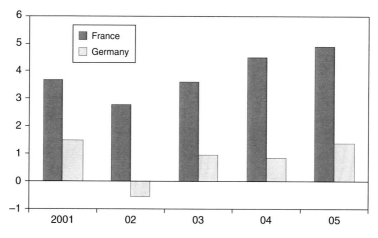

Source: IMF staff calculations.

Figure 5.8 Real Export Growth, 2001–05 to 2006–10 *(Percent)*

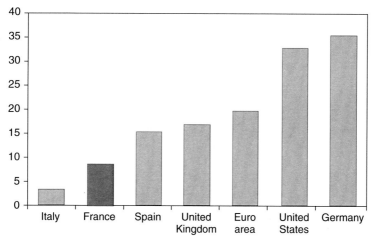

Source: IMF staff calculations.
Note: Percentage change of average export volumes between two periods.

its peers. Moreover, its loss of market share in the euro area is noteworthy, given that the area accounts for about half of France's total exports. During the latter half of the 2000s, France lost about 1½ percentage points of market share in the euro area, compared to a ¼ percentage point loss for Germany.

A key factor behind this weakening of competitiveness has been a larger gap between wage growth and total factor productivity (TFP) growth relative to neighboring countries since the mid-2000s (Figure 5.9). In particular, relative to Germany, French wages grew much faster, while TFP growth lagged for more than a decade. Traditional price-based indicators are insufficient to explain

Figure 5.9   Wage Growth Minus Total Factor Productivity Growth *(Percent)*

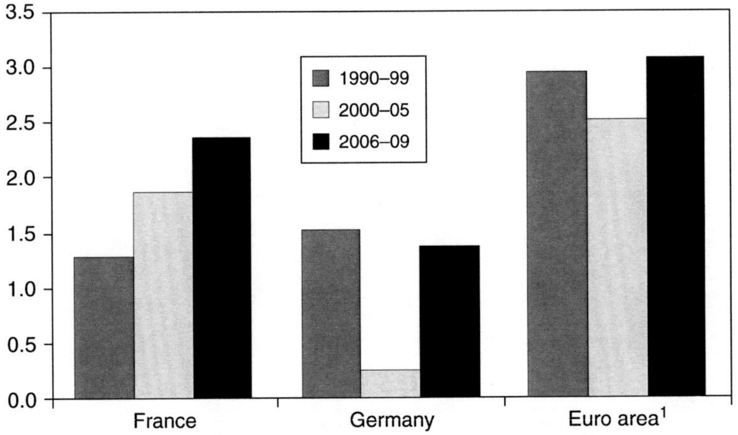

Sources: The Conference Board Total Economy Database, January 2011.
www.conferenceboard.org/data/economydatabase/; and the Organization for Economic Cooperation and Development
(OECD).
[1]OECD countries excluding Germany and France.

France's weaker export performance. Since the mid-2000s, all countries in the euro area experienced a real appreciation relative to the United States in terms of the consumer-price-index-based real effective exchange rate (REER), mainly due to the appreciation of the euro. However, relative to the other core countries in the euro area (Germany, Italy, and Spain), France lost competitiveness only to Germany in terms of REER, export prices, unit labor costs, and labor productivity (Figure 5.10). In contrast, France experienced a smaller real appreciation, a slower increase in export prices and unit labor costs, and a faster increase in labor productivity than Italy and Spain (Figure 5.11). This implies that nonprice factors, which are related to structural issues, are likely to have contributed to the underperformance of the French export sector.[7]

French exports have faced stronger competition from emerging market economies than have the exports of France's large euro-area peers. French exports consist of some high-tech products (aeronautics and pharmacy), but also contain a large share of low- to medium-tech products that face competition from both industrialized and emerging market economies.[8] Although France's exports to fast-growing emerging market and developing economies have increased significantly during the last decade, its export growth to these destinations has lagged behind that of the other euro-area countries. France has also lost market share in fast-growing sectors, including some of its large export sectors, in marked contrast to Germany.

_____

[7]Cheng (2010) also found that traditional price and foreign demand factors can only partly explain the decline of the market share of French exports during the 2000s, suggesting that nonprice factors may have played a significant role in the competitiveness loss.
[8]For more details, see European Commission (2010).

Figure 5.10 Real Effective Exchange Rate *(Index based on the consumer price index; 1999 = 100)*

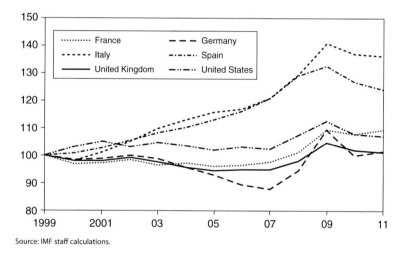

Source: IMF, Global Data Sources.

Figure 5.11 Unit Labor Costs, Manufacturing Sector *(Index; 1999 = 100)*

Source: IMF staff calculations.

The underperformance of the French export sector also reflects labor and product market rigidities. Labor market rigidities have restricted firms' flexibility to adjust to the changing economic environment. A high level of employment protection, high minimum wage, and one of the highest labor tax wedges among member countries of the Organization for Economic Cooperation and Development (OECD),[9] among other factors, have led to high unemployment and lower working hours, contributing to low labor input (Figure 5.12). OECD estimates

[9]Earlier reforms aimed at reducing employer-paid social security contributions for low wage levels (between 1 and 1.6 times the minimum wage) have significantly lowered the tax wedge at the bottom of the income distribution.

Figure 5.12 Employment Protection, 2008 *(Index)*

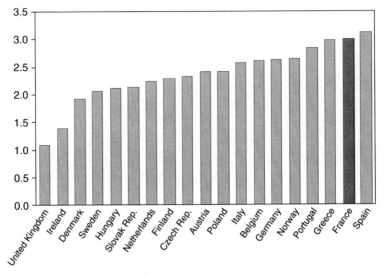

Source: Organization for Economic Cooperation and Development.
Note: A high reading implies high levels of employment protection.

Figure 5.13 Product Market Regulation, 2008 *(Index)*

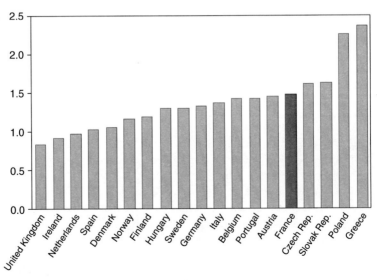

Source: Organization for Economic Cooperation and Development.
Note: A high reading implies high levels of regulation.

show that France's product market policies have also inhibited competition relative to its EMU peers (Figure 5.13).[10] These rigidities have led to loss of efficiency, inability to make a breakthrough in new markets, insufficient research and innovation, and a loss of technological edge, contributing to the underperformance of France's export sector.[11]

ARE FRANCE'S IMBALANCES A PROBLEM?

While a moderate current account deficit does not pose risks, it is not desirable at this stage for France. At about 2 percent of GDP in 2011, France's current account deficit is not excessively large. However, given demographic factors, it is not desirable for France to maintain current account deficits for extended periods. In addition, given the need for fiscal consolidation, maintaining strong growth would require a larger contribution from external demand by restoring competitiveness. Also, since lower potential growth and loss of competitiveness share common underlying factors, addressing potential growth would lead to higher welfare for the French population, while also helping to reduce the external imbalance.

Market concerns pertaining to France's fiscal position and public debt rose amid the intensification of the euro-area crisis in 2011, with a widening of bond spreads relative to German bunds and rising credit default swap spreads. Financial stability concerns have abated considerably since then, with a marked decline of interest rate spreads vis-à-vis Germany, but the experience highlights the importance of the sustainability of public debt in terms of financial stability. High public debt levels reduce policy space to deal with future shocks and can crowd out private investment, lowering growth prospects. Also, as higher public debt inevitably implies a higher tax burden in the future, given the already high level of French tax rates, it could create other distortions, undermining ongoing efforts to revitalize the economy.

France's external and internal imbalances should be viewed with care. France is the second biggest economy in the euro area. A credit event in the French debt market or a loss of investor confidence in the creditworthiness of the sovereign could have significant wider repercussions for other sovereigns (including for the European Financial Stability Facility/European Stability Mechanism, which is critical for managing the ongoing euro-area crisis) as well as for corporate spreads. Also, given the close interlinkages between the real and financial sectors, the risks of contagion are high, as evident from the sovereign debt crisis in euro-area periphery countries.

In sum, financial instability in France could have large cross-border spillovers. French banks have large cross-border exposures to the euro-area countries under IMF programs or are experiencing heightened market scrutiny. Thus, intensified market pressures on euro-area periphery banks could affect the balance sheets of French banks.

---

[10]Kabundi and Nadal De-Simone (2009) find that adjustment to a negative cost shock tends to be more via quantities than via prices, pointing to an insufficient flexibility of labor and product markets.

[11]See Hallaert (2012a) for further discussion on the structural factors that have affected France's export performance.

HOW TO ADDRESS IMBALANCES

Domestic Priorities

Sustaining fiscal consolidation over the medium term is needed to keep public finances on a sustainable path, while longstanding structural reforms should be implemented to boost competitiveness and growth. The external and fiscal imbalances are closely interlinked. A more competitive and growth-oriented economy is essential not only for keeping external balances in check, but also for achieving sustainable public finances. Fiscal policy that puts public finances on such a sustainable path, combined with growth-friendly tax reform, could usefully support growth- and competitiveness-enhancing structural reform policies and help contain external imbalances by ensuring an improved public saving–investment balance.[12]

Anchoring Fiscal Sustainability

A key policy priority is keeping public debt on a sustainable track. To abide by the terms under the second EDP, the authorities have committed to ambitious fiscal deficit targets to reduce the fiscal deficit to 3 percent of GDP by 2013 and 2.2 percent by 2014. According to an IMF staff assessment, there would be a shortfall of about 0.5 percent of GDP due to somewhat optimistic growth projections, requiring additional measures from 2013 onward to meet the fiscal targets and to maintain public debt on a sustainable path (IMF, 2012). Failing to implement such additional measures would result in higher public debt ratios (about 91 percent of GDP, as projected by IMF staff). Previous consolidation experience highlights that strong political will and a shared resolve for consolidation at all levels of government, including local governments and the social security system, are critical factors for the success of fiscal consolidation. In the event of lower-than-expected growth, the authorities should allow the automatic stabilizers to operate fully and focus on a deficit target in structural terms.

To achieve the fiscal targets for 2013 and 2014 without undermining incentives to work and invest, it is necessary to achieve greater fiscal adjustment, beyond what is currently envisaged. Second, the composition of adjustment could be strengthened by rebalancing the fiscal effort toward expenditure containment. A more ambitious expenditure reduction over the medium term would also help enable a gradual reduction of the tax burden, which is already among the highest in Europe, and strengthen incentives to work and invest. Expenditure containment should involve all levels of government, based on a rationalization of spending. The initiatives taken by the government to improve the efficiency of public spending and initiate stricter ex ante evaluation of public investment projects need to be accompanied by a better match between resources and mandates across

---

[12]Policy recommendations are based on the IMF's 2011 and 2012 Article IV discussions (IMF, 2011a; IMF, 2012).

the various levels of government, strict management of health spending, and tighter controls over the wage bill of all government institutions.

France's Organic Law, which transposes the European Fiscal Compact into French law, would contribute to enhancing fiscal policy credibility. Through its built-in fiscal rule and corrective mechanism, the Organic Law will anchor annual budgetary policies more firmly into a medium-term objective of budget balance. Establishing the High Council of Public Finances to provide independent macro-economic projections and monitor implementation of corrective actions in the event of deviations from the established fiscal trajectory would enhance the credibility of the multi-year budget.

Furthermore, to ensure long-term sustainability, deeper reforms of key pension and health care parameters are also needed. On the pension side, further increasing the legal retirement age in line with life expectancy would prevent continued increases in time spent in retirement as medical advances continue to lengthen life spans.[13] On the health care front, as the rise in living standards and technical progress will continue to put pressure on public expenditures, continued efficiency gains are necessary, in addition to initiation of a planned reform of long-term care in 2012, to prevent an unsustainable rise in health and long-term care spending. It should be noted, however, that France is among the lower- to medium-risk countries in terms of future health care costs, with the projected increase of annual spending on public health being lower than the European average over the next 20 years.[14]

Financial stability concerns abated considerably in mid-2012, but international regulatory changes could still result in significant adjustment costs. French banks have improved their solvency ratios and funding structures through retained earnings and disposal of international noncore businesses, and are currently well positioned to comply with Basel III capital requirements. However, international regulatory changes—more stringent liquidity requirements for banks and new regulations and accounting standards for insurance companies—would make it costlier to provide long-term financing. The overhaul of the financial taxation of savings envisaged by the government should be an important instrument to address this challenge by creating a more level playing field among financial instruments and by increasing incentives for long-term saving.

Enhancing Competitiveness

To keep external imbalances in check, France needs to improve its competitiveness by pursuing structural reforms to increase TFP while moderating wage growth. France's lagging export performance over the past decade indicates the importance of strengthening competitiveness. The latest overall exchange rate assessment suggests the possibility of some overvaluation of the REER, indicating

---

[13]The 2003 pension reform linked the contribution years for a full pension to life expectancy.
[14]See the IMF's April 2011 *Fiscal Monitor* for details (IMF, 2011b).

that the need for wage moderation and cost containment is especially important given that France is a member of a currency union. To address nonprice factors that have played significant roles in the underperformance of France's export sector, it is important to pursue comprehensive structural reform strategies in the product market, labor market, and tax area.

The reform strategy in product markets should be focused on promoting innovation and creating favorable conditions for business. Enhancing competitiveness by lowering regulatory restrictions would help increase productivity and employment. In this context, the easing of regulatory entry barriers to the services sector, including professional services, would raise value added in the services sector but also have positive spillovers to the manufacturing sector by reducing costs of key inputs.[15]

Labor market reform should focus on increasing labor market participation and reabsorbing the unemployed. Although welcome progress has been made to reabsorb the unemployed by providing appropriate incentives for both firms and job-seekers—including by simplifying layoff procedures and enhancing work-study schemes—more efforts are needed. Easing high levels of employment protection would provide appropriate incentives for firms to create more jobs, and reducing the comparatively long duration of unemployment benefits or lowering benefit levels over time could strengthen incentives for people to look for jobs and increase the effective labor supply.

Labor market participation of young and low-skilled workers as well as seniors needs to be increased (Table 5.1). The high minimum wage (*salaire minimum interprofessionnel de croissance* – SMIC) has priced low-skilled workers out of the labor market, especially the young. To increase labor demand for these groups, it is important to continue to limit the increase of the SMIC, for example by reviewing the indexation formula, which is currently partly based on inflation. To increase the labor force participation of seniors (among the lowest in Europe), it is important to continue the phasing out of pre-retirement benefits, relax constraints on combining employment and retirement benefits, and undertake pension reforms.

Reform of labor and business income taxation would improve incentives for employment and growth. Lowering the labor tax wedge, which remains high on average relative to the other OECD countries, could increase labor demand while preventing higher wage claims by unions. Reforms of the tax-benefit system targeting work incentives to the high labor supply margins—senior workers and women with school-age children—are expected to be effective and cost-efficient.[16] Notwithstanding the already-existing social benefit (*Revenu de Solidarité Active* – RSA) and tax credit (*Prime pour l'emploi* – PPE) that encourage labor supply, more generous earned income tax credits and special credit for social security

---

[15]See Hallaert (2012b) for a discussion on potential gains from services sector deregulation.
[16]While the employment rate of prime-aged women (30–54 years) has increased in line with that of other OECD countries, the average hours worked by French women have declined markedly since the late 1970s. See Poirson (2011).

TABLE 5.1

Employment Ratios			
	Total[1]	Women[2]	Older workers[3]
	2011	2011	2011
Belgium	62.5	56.7	38.7
Finland	70.5	67.5	57.0
France	64.3	59.7	41.4
Germany	74.0	67.7	59.9
Greece	56.6	45.1	39.4
Ireland	61.1	56.0	50.8
Italy	57.9	46.5	37.9
Netherlands	76.1	69.9	56.1
Portugal	68.2	60.4	47.9
Spain	59.0	52.8	44.5
United Kingdom	72.6	65.3	56.8
United States	70.0	62.0	60.0
OECD countries	67.5	56.7	54.4

Source: Organization for Economic Cooperation and Development (OECD).
[1]Percent of working-age population.
[2]Percent of female population (15–64).
[3]Percent of population age 55–64.

contributions paid for these groups of workers could be considered. A corporate tax reform, by lowering the statutory rate along with broadening the tax base and reducing complexity, would help make the system fairer and simpler and make the corporate tax system less biased against small firms, which are often the source of innovation and job creation. Reducing the relatively large bias toward debt financing from interest deductibility would reduce banks' excess leverage and promote greater reliance on equity finance, which could ultimately boost innovative investments.

TOWARD GLOBAL ACTION

With respect to global rebalancing and collective action, France needs to take the following steps:

- *Additional fiscal consolidation to firmly place public finances on a sustainable track.* The announced fiscal measures in the pipeline are based on relatively optimistic growth projections, so additional measures are needed to meet the deficit target under the EDP by 2013, and further fiscal consolidation would be needed to achieve fiscal sustainability as targeted in the Stability Program. The consolidation could be financed by expenditure cuts and additional revenue measures, including an increase in value-added tax (VAT) revenue.

- *Tax reform to reduce distortions and raise potential output.* The corporate income tax could be lowered to raise investment and potential output. Labor taxation could also be reduced to increase labor participation. These tax and social security contribution cuts could be financed with further increases in VAT revenue and a cut in tax expenditures.

• *Structural reforms to boost productivity in nontradables, together with wage moderation.*[17] Product market reforms to boost productivity, particularly in services, could include convergence of regulation in network industries, retail trade, and professional services to standards for best practices. Additional labor market reforms and minimum wage moderation are also crucial to improve productivity and reduce unemployment (notably of the young and low-skilled workers).

REFERENCES

Cheng, Kevin, 2010, "Developments in France's External Competitiveness—An Update," in *France: Selected Issues Paper*, IMF Country Report No. 10/243 (Washington: International Monetary Fund).

European Commission, 2010, "Surveillance of Intra-Euro-Area Competitiveness and Imbalances," *European Economy* 1 (May) (Brussels: European Commission Directorate General for Economic and Financial Affairs).

Hallaert, Jean-Jacques, 2012a, "Structural Reforms and Export Performance," in *France: Selected Issues Paper*, IMF Country Report (Washington: International Monetary Fund).

———, 2012b, "Gains from Service Sector Deregulation," in *France: Selected Issues Paper*, IMF Country Report (Washington: International Monetary Fund).

International Monetary Fund (IMF), 2011a, "France—Staff Report for the 2011 Article IV Consultation," IMF Country Report No. 11/121 (Washington: International Monetary Fund).

———, 2011b, *Fiscal Monitor: Shifting Gears: Tackling Challenges on the Road to Fiscal Adjustment*, April (Washington: International Monetary Fund).

———, 2012, "France—Staff Report for the 2012 Article IV Consultation," IMF Country Report (Washington: International Monetary Fund).

Kabundi, Alain, and Francisco Nadal De-Simone, 2009, "Recent French Export Performance: Is there a Competitiveness Problem?" IMF Working Paper 09/2 (Washington: International Monetary Fund).

Martin, Edouard, Irina Tytell, and Irina Yakadina, 2011, "France: Lessons from Past Fiscal Consolidation Plans," IMF Working Paper 11/89 (Washington: International Monetary Fund).

Poirson, Hélène, 2011, "Toward a Growth-Oriented Tax System for France," in *France: Selected Issues Paper*, IMF Country Report 11/212 (Washington: International Monetary Fund).

---

[17]The structural reform scenario was developed in close partnership with the OECD, which provided estimates of the impact of structural reforms on productivity.

CHAPTER 6

India: Dealing with Perennial Fiscal Deficits

MITALI DAS[1]

India's fiscal imbalances have remained large despite a sustained period of high economic growth. Large budget deficits and high public debt can be traced to a political economy that exerts strong pressure on spending, a weak revenue system, and financial restrictions that permit weak fiscal balances to persist with little market stress. At the same time, high growth and favorable demographics have caused private saving to surge. The perpetuation of fiscal imbalances poses risks for macroeconomic stability, as evident from recent developments in major advanced economies. Fiscal adjustment is needed to reduce imbalances and sustain growth.

Widespread economic reforms following an external crisis in 1991 ushered in an era of impressive growth in India. Widening fiscal and external deficits came to the fore in 1991 when a rapid deterioration in public finances, coupled with an oil price shock and heightened political uncertainty, resulted in a classic balance of payments crisis. The postcrisis adjustment—which included a wide spectrum of fiscal, financial sector, and capital account reforms aimed at reducing government control, cutting back on the red tape required to operate a business, and providing a larger role for market forces—raised the potential for higher growth. Real output growth, which had averaged an annual rate of 4½ percent from 1976–91, rose to an annual average of 6 percent from 1992–99. Growth then edged higher, to an average 7.2 percent between 2000 and the run-up to the global financial crisis (Figure 6.1). The crisis only modestly slowed this momentum, as output continued to grow in excess of 6 percent each year from 2008–11.

Despite highly favorable growth-interest differentials, fiscal imbalances have remained large. General government deficits averaged 7.7 percent of GDP between 1992 and 2007 (Figure 6.2). Primary deficits were lower, averaging 2.4 percent, but large enough to result in a steady increase of over 14 percentage points in the gross public debt ratio from 1995–2003, peaking at 84.3 percent in 2003. A sustained consolidation effort, including the adoption of fiscal rules in 2003, put fiscal positions on the mend in the years preceding the crisis. But fiscal imbalances deteriorated again with the onset of the crisis.

[1]Mitali Das is a Senior Economist in the IMF Research Department. This chapter was written with guidance from Josh Felman, input from Michal Andrle, and support from Eric Bang, David Reichsfeld, and Anne Lalramnghakhleli Moses.

Figure 6.1   India: Real GDP Growth *(Percent)*

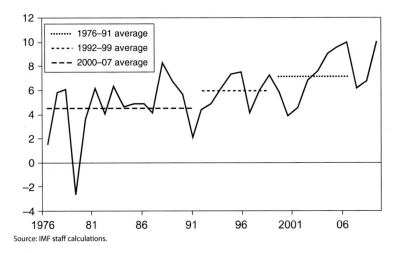

Source: IMF staff calculations.

Figure 6.2   India: Debt Dynamics *(In percent)*

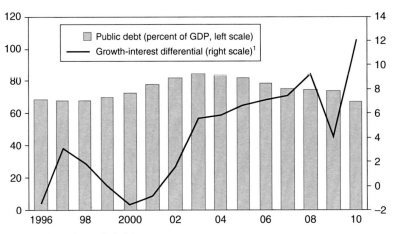

Sources: CEIC; and IMF staff calculations.
[1]The differential, in percentage points, is real GDP growth less real yields on 10-year government bonds (calculated using the GDP deflator).

After a modest improvement for a few years following the country's 1991 economic crisis, fiscal positions worsened through the early 2000s. The revenue share of GDP stayed broadly flat over the 1990s, while the expenditure share was on a mild upward trend. Thereafter, despite significant improvement in revenue collection, which rose some 2.1 percentage points of GDP from 1998–2004, expenditures rose nearly in parallel, owing to rising interest payments and unrelenting increases in subsidies, wages, pension payments, and defense spending. A strong effort at fiscal tightening then helped lower deficits and the debt ratio. Following government passage of the Fiscal Responsibility and Budget

Figure 6.3 India: General Government Finances *(Percent of GDP)*

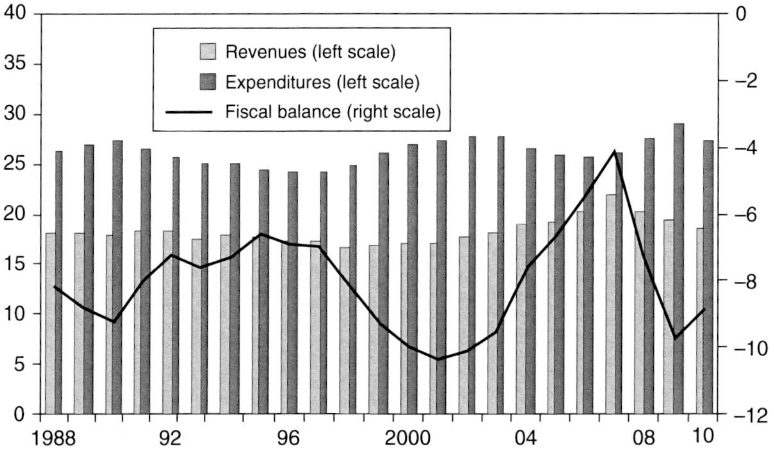

Source: IMF staff calculations.

Management Act (FRBMA) in 2003, public debt receded nearly 10 percentage points between 2004 and 2008 to 74.7 percent of GDP in 2008, assisted by a brief surplus in the primary balance and sizable growth-interest differentials.

Progress with deficit reduction reversed following the global financial crisis. A combination of spending measures introduced prior to the crisis, a soaring subsidy bill, a large fiscal stimulus, and a cyclical downturn in revenues widened the overall deficit from 4.2 percent of GDP in 2007 to over 9 percent in 2009 (Figure 6.3). However, a spike in the growth-interest differential, reflecting the swift recovery and low real interest rates, helped keep the growth of public debt in check. It fell to 67.3 percent in 2010, but remained highest among the G20 emerging market economies.

Large public dissaving and high investment needs have kept the external position in modest deficit despite a secular increase in private saving. In particular, national saving and investment have evolved on parallel trajectories, each only modestly rising between 1985 and the late 1990s, before escalating sharply through 2009. Trends in national saving and investment have been driven overwhelmingly by private sector behavior.

Private sector investment boomed following the economic reforms of the 1990s, while public sector investment declined sharply (over 4 percentage points of GDP from 1991–2001), particularly in much-needed infrastructure investment, as a result of the government's early efforts at deficit reduction (Figure 6.4). Public sector capital expenditures rose modestly over 2001–09, but have played a negligible role in the dramatic rise in national investment. Although private gross investment is relatively high,[2] private sector participation in the critical area of infrastructure

---

[2]India's private investment rate is the highest among emerging G20 economies (and other economies at a similar level of per capita income). Among emerging G20 economies, India's national investment rate is second to that of China.

Figure 6.4 India: Investment *(Percent of GDP)*

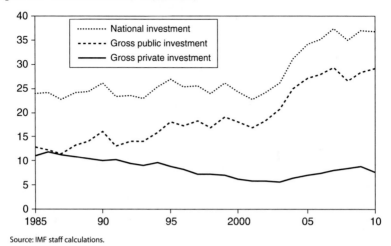

Source: IMF staff calculations.

Figure 6.5 India: Saving *(Percent of GDP)*

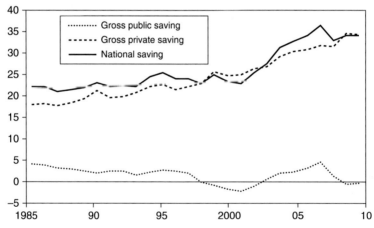

Source: IMF staff calculations.

development has been disappointing in the past, owing to a combination of limited financial sector deepening, capital controls, and governance problems.[3]

The surge in private saving has been led by the household sector. An era of high-income growth combined with the life-cycle implications of a rising working-age population has resulted in a rapid increase in household saving rates, which rose 10 percentage points as a share of GDP between 1991 and 2009 to reach 24 percent (Figure 6.5). Corporate gross saving rose as well by about 5 percentage points in this period, reflecting improved profitability following the

[3]However, during the first half of the Eleventh Five-Year Plan (2007–12), private sector participation in infrastructure investment exceeded plan projections.

Figure 6.6 India: Financial Surplus by Sector *(Percent of GDP)*

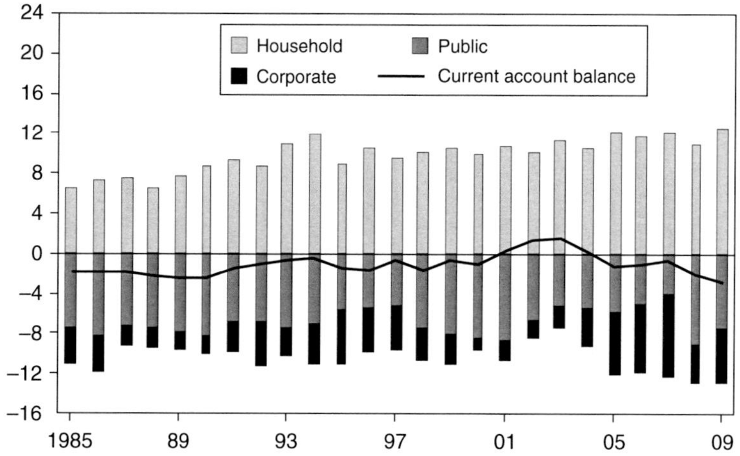

Sources: CEIC; and IMF staff calculations.

financial reforms of the 1990s (Figure 6.6). Corporate *excess* saving (gross corporate saving less corporate investment), though, remained negative, as private investment boomed. At 34 percent of GDP in 2010, India's private saving rate was second to China among G20 economies.

Risks of perpetuating imbalances over the medium term are high. With growth projected to remain robust and the government's announced commitment toward fiscal consolidation, IMF staff's baseline projection is for the public debt ratio to fall about 5 percentage points between 2010 and 2016 to 62 percent, in line with authorities' targets.[4] However, risks to this forecast are high, stemming from pressures for social spending and infrastructure investment, inertia in withdrawing fiscal stimulus, and continued delays in planned tax reforms. IMF staff project that high growth and favorable demographics will push private saving rates higher in the medium term, to 37 percent of GDP by 2016.

ROOT CAUSES OF IMBALANCES

Root causes of fiscal imbalances can be traced to political economy factors that exert strong pressure on spending and resistance to raising taxes, a weak revenue system, and government regulations that permit fiscal excesses to be financed with little market stress. Rapid growth and favorable demographics underlie private saving imbalances, while missing insurance markets also play a role. The factors behind each of India's major imbalances are described below.

---

[4]See India Article IV Staff Report (IMF, 2012).

Fiscal Imbalances

The rising share of expenditure in GDP through the late 1990s and early 2000s and then again in the years before the global financial crisis—without a commensurate increase in the revenue share of GDP—reflects the failure of the government to take advantage of a sustained boom to build fiscal space. On the expenditure side, major factors include large outlays on subsidies, due in part to of a high incidence of poverty, a succession of coalition governments, and federal-state fiscal arrangements. The key factor on the revenue side is a complex and outdated tax code. High private saving, capital controls, and statutory purchase of government securities by financial institutions combine to provide stable and relatively low-cost financing for public debt.

The benefits of greater economic prosperity have accrued unevenly, resulting in persistent pressure to increase government social spending. India's social indicators compare unfavorably regionally as well as with other G20 emerging market economies. In particular, while India's poverty rates have declined over the past two decades, the World Bank estimates that 42 percent of the population (410 million people) remained impoverished as of 2005 (Table 6.1).[5] As a consequence, there is persistent political pressure to increase social spending and subsidize commodities (notably fuel and food). Subsidy spending accounted for 2.1 percent of GDP in 2009, almost as much as expenditures on all of health and rural development. Meanwhile, the expansion of safety nets in recent years has resulted in a steady increase in nonsubsidy social expenditures as well, which accounted for 3.1 percent of GDP in 2009.

Rising expenditures are partly a result of an era of coalition governments. Since the mid-1990s, as regional parties with diverse regional interests have strengthened, the central government has had to depend on coalitions of as many as 16 distinct political parties to stay in power. Catering to a wide range of ideologies and constituencies has necessitated fiscal forbearance and made it politically more difficult to withdraw or reform populist schemes such as subsidized commodities and cheap

TABLE 6.1

India's Social Indicators Compared with Other G20 Emerging Market Economies (Percent)			
	Poverty[1]	**Malnutrition[2]**	**Employment[3]**
Argentina	0.87	2.3	56.5
Brazil	3.8	2.2	63.9
China	15.92	4.5	71.0
India	**41.64**	**43.5**	**55.6**
Indonesia	19.73	3.4	61.8
Mexico	3.44	5.3	57.1
Russia	0	n.a	56.7
Saudi Arabia	n.a	5.3	47.2
Africa	17.35	n.a	41.1
Turkey	2.72	n.a	42.3

Source: World Bank.
[1]Percent of population earning less than $1.25 a day at purchasing power parity.
[2]Percent of children malnourished, weight for age (under five years old).
[3]Percent of population aged 15+.

---

[5]Using the World Bank indicator of poverty based on the headcount of persons (percent of population) earning less than $1.25 a day at purchasing power parity.

Figure 6.7   India: Central Government and State Shares in Government Gross Deficits *(Percent)*

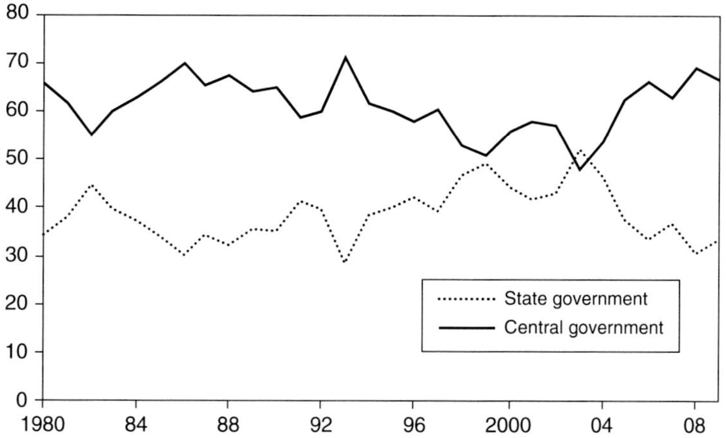

Sources: CEIC; and IMF staff calculations.
Note: The gross fiscal deficit is defined here by total expenditure, inclusive of net loans, minus revenue and nondebt capital
      receipts.

electric power, which have often been poorly targeted. Moreover, implementation of social assistance programs has been inefficient, resulting in significant leakage and the denial of benefits to eligible persons (Comptroller and Auditor General of India, 2008). This reflects the absence of a system of unique identification or national registers (that is only now being gradually implemented) and poor enforcement.

The federal-state tax and spending structure has made it difficult to enforce fiscal discipline. Under India's fiscal federalism, about two-thirds of tax revenue is collected by the central government, while states are tasked with carrying out a similar proportion of general government expenditures—using tax-sharing and transfers from the central government—to implement government policies.[6] With implicit central government guarantees on state government debt, the system offers a high degree of autonomy to states but few incentives to maintain fiscal restraint (since the mid-2000s, a majority of states have adopted their own fiscal responsibility rules).

During the 1990s, deteriorating general government balances reflected rising fiscal excesses at the state level. In particular, the trend decline in central tax collection over the 1990s led to a reduction in transfers to states. However, states not only failed to raise their own revenues, but also retained a high level of spending.[7] Consequently, their contribution to the general government deficit rose from 35 percent in 1992 to nearly 50 percent in 1999 (Figure 6.7).

---

[6]The share of central government revenues transferred to states changes over time. It is set by the Finance Commission, a constitutional body that meets every five years with the primary purpose of determining the sharing of centrally collected tax proceeds between the central and state governments, and the distribution of grants-in-aid of revenue across states.
[7]Both central and state budget deficits rose in part due to the large wage increases recommended by the Fifth Pay Commission.

Figure 6.8 General Government Revenues among G20 Emerging Market Economies, 2010 *(Percent of GDP)*

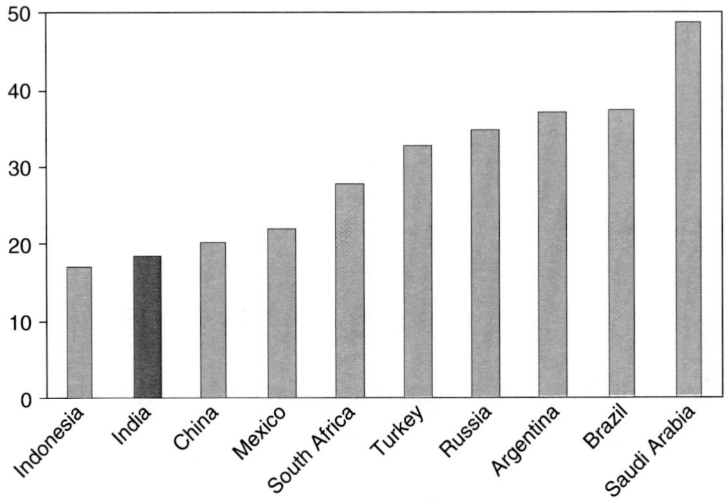

Source: IMF staff calculations.

Differences in tax collection responsibilities partially explain the varying evolutions of central and state government fiscal deficits. The central government is assigned tax collection for customs and excise duties, from which it draws its largest share of revenues, while states collect taxes on commodities and services, which constitute the preponderance of state revenues. This system has meant that both the economic cycle and structural changes (e.g., in demand for commodities) have played a role in determining the evolution of central versus state government deficits.

A narrow tax base, poor compliance, and weak collection efforts have eroded tax revenues. A comparison of general government revenues across emerging G20 economies indicates that India (with a 2010 revenue share of GDP equal to 18.5 percent) is at the bottom end in revenue collection (Figure 6.8).[8] In part, this reflects the low buoyancy of the tax system, which is narrowly based on indirect taxes and manufacturing activity, with agriculture and the rapidly growing services sector largely outside the tax net. It also reflects weak enforcement, extensive loopholes, and political resistance to raising taxes in a still-poor economy.

Incomplete tax reforms after the external payments crisis contributed to declining revenues over the course of the 1990s. Revenue collection dropped by 1.6 percentage points of GDP from 1992–99, even as household and corporate incomes surged. In part, this reflected the impact of trade and financial liberalization reforms, which narrowed the tax base by cutting trade tax rates and customs

---

[8]India's revenue share of GDP fell in the lower third of the distribution each year from 2007–10 among economies whose nominal U.S. dollar GDP per capita was between $648 and $1,488 in those years.

duties, but without (planned but not implemented) compensating hikes in direct taxes and measures to reduce exemptions and loopholes.

Income tax revenues have been stagnant due to constant adaptation of exemption levels and income brackets. Despite a highly progressive income tax code, and private nominal incomes that escalated sevenfold from 1991–2008, the share of personal income tax revenues in GDP remained very low, exceeding no more than 3.6 percent of GDP.[9] While any explanation must include low compliance, political economy played a significant role. In particular, the tax schedule was changed repeatedly, with continuous increases in exemption thresholds and income brackets (Piketty and Qian, 2009). Notably, the rise in thresholds was almost as large as the rise in nominal income growth itself. As a result, the population subject to income tax rose modestly, from about 1 percent in 1991 to 3 percent in 2008 (Piketty and Qian, 2009). This is a reflection of strong political resistance to taxation given the still-high incidence of poverty, and the ineffectiveness of tax policy given the very large share of informal workers.

Financial Controls

High levels of private saving, capital controls, and statutory requirements for investing in government securities have allowed for financing fiscal deficits without discernible market stress. Despite major financial sector reforms starting in the 1990s, the government's statutory liquidity ratio (SLR) currently requires banks to hold one-fourth of their deposits in the form of government or other approved securities,[10] while insurance and provident funds are also subject to similar investment regulations. In combination with capital controls and an increasingly large pool of household saving, this system has provided a stable and relatively low-cost source of funds for financing government debt. Indeed, from 2001–07, on average, 50 percent of household saving was used to finance fiscal deficits (Figure 6.9). Moreover, regulatory requirements that direct private sector resources toward the purchase of government securities have hindered development of the corporate debt market.

High administered interest rates on small saving schemes have reinforced the effects of statutory requirements on banks. Small saving schemes are government-operated deposits in post offices and provident funds that are used exclusively to finance government debt (Figure 6.10).[11] The need to ensure adequate resources to finance the government's large borrowing has kept (administratively set) interest rates on these schemes high.[12]

---

[9]IMF staff estimates using data from the World Economic Outlook and CEIC databases, calculated as the ratio of direct taxes paid by households and miscellaneous receipts of government to GDP.
[10]As part of financial sector reforms in the 1990s, the SLR was progressively reduced from 38.5 percent in 1991 to 25 percent in 1995. In December 2010 it was lowered to 24 percent.
[11]These schemes drew about 21 percent of aggregate bank deposits from 2000–08 and provided an average of 16 percent of funding for government debt in this period. Meanwhile, public sector debt to foreign creditors peaked at 37 percent of GDP during the external payments crisis, declined thereafter, and is virtually absent presently. The only external debt the public sector has currently is to multilateral institutions.
[12]In Figure 6.10, market borrowing refers to bank bond purchases under the SLR.

Figure 6.9   India: Use of Household Financial Saving *(Percent of household financial saving)*

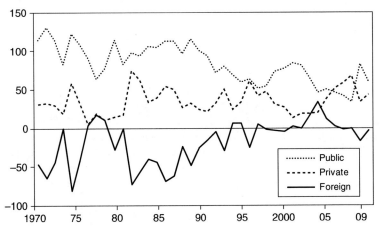

Sources: CEIC; and IMF staff calculations.
Note: Public and private investment are in net terms (investment less saving). "Foreign" is the current account balance.

Figure 6.10   India: Financing of Government Debt *(Average percent share over 2000–08)*

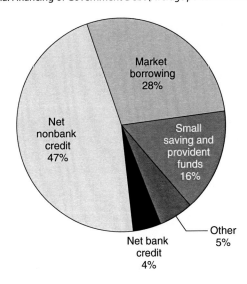

Source: CEIC.

These high interest rates on small saving schemes have also distorted lending and borrowing behavior in the banking sector. In effect, they force banks to keep their deposit rates high and, thus, lending rates high as well (Figure 6.11). For borrowers, this has served to dampen credit demand, particularly for small and medium-sized enterprises (SMEs), which have few financing options beyond bank credit.

Figure 6.11 India: Lending and Deposit Rates in Commercial Banks and Small Saving Schemes *(Percent)*

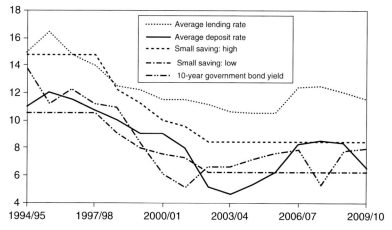

Sources: CEIC; Reserve Bank of India; and IMF staff calculations.

TABLE 6.2

India: Commercial Banks' Holdings of Securities *(Percent of deposits)*		
	Goverment securities	**Other securities**
1996–99	32.6	5.6
2000–05	39.1	2.1
2006–07	32.1	0.6
2008–10	30.9	0.2

Source: CEIC.

Finally, SLRs and high administered rates on small saving schemes, in conjunction with inadequate improvement in the financial sector's risk assessment framework, have resulted in perpetuating distortive financial restrictions. In particular, while economic reforms in the 1990s improved competitiveness, they also raised the risks of lending, without an accompanying increase in banks' capacity to evaluate or handle these risks (Banerjee and Duflo, 2002; Singh and Srinivasan, 2005). As a result, in periods of high administered rates (and consequently high bank lending and deposit rates), investment in government securities has provided a relatively attractive and less-risky alternative than providing credit to the private sector, given the lack of opportunities for investing in corporate bonds and external capital controls that limit investment abroad (Table 6.2).[13] This confluence of distortions created by the SLR and high administered rates, along with very gradual improvement in banks' regulatory framework, has contributed

---

[13]Investment in government securities has the added advantage of having a low risk rating in meeting capital adequacy requirements.

to sustained periods of "lazy banking," reducing banks' role in financial intermediation.[14] In addition, it has raised interest rate risk due to a significant maturity mismatch in banks' balance sheets.

Private Saving Imbalances

The surge in household saving reflects the dramatic rise in disposable incomes and a rise in the working-age ratio. Household saving rates in India have been on the rise for over four decades, increasing steadily from 9 percent of GDP in 1970 to nearly 24 percent in 2009.[15] High growth has boosted household incomes beyond subsistence consumption levels. Indeed, personal disposable income nearly tripled in real terms over 1991–2008. As many households' incomes surpassed their subsistence levels of consumption, household saving ratios increased (Figure 6.12). As a result, the real private consumption share of real GDP has been in steady decline, falling from 69 percent in 1991 to 59 percent in 2010. Even so, real private consumption grew at a robust annual rate of 6 percent during this period.

Figure 6.12 India: Private Disposable Income and Consumption *(Billions of 2005 rupees)*

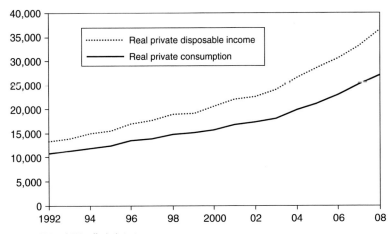

Sources: CEIC; and IMF staff calculations.

---

[14]While the 1990s reforms reduced the SLR from nearly 40 percent to 25 percent, banks' investment in government securities has since systematically surpassed these requirements, notably in long-maturity government bonds. In part, some excess holding of government securities could be due to banks' liquidity needs, given that the SLR cannot be used to obtain liquidity from the Reserve Bank of India. More recently, holdings above the SLRs could be due to an upward shift in the yield curve, which may have discouraged banks from unwinding such holdings as that would have resulted in losses being crystallized. However, these are unlikely to be a complete explanation, given that banks have held as much as 40 percent of deposits in government securities, including in periods (e.g., 2003) when bond yields remained largely flat.

[15]IMF staff analysis suggests that demographic, socioeconomic, and macroeconomic variables partially explain India's high private saving rate (IMF, 2010). These empirical estimates do not explicitly take into account whether the lack of insurance affects private saving.

At the same time, a significant rise in the working-age dependency ratio has contributed to high saving rates. India is in the midst of a demographic transition that has lifted the share of the working-age population from 58 to 64 percent over the last two decades. The observed rise in household saving thus conforms to the predictions of the life-cycle hypothesis.

Inadequate insurance vehicles and limited access to credit have played a role in the accumulation of household saving. Households and SMEs face barriers to obtaining credit, which has contributed to the high rate of saving. Moreover, a poorly developed and state-dominated system of life insurance and a nascent private health insurance industry, combined with little scope for provident saving for informal workers, forces households to save. However, as these factors have been in place for decades, they are not an explanation for the escalation in household saving rates.

Corporate saving has also played a role in rising private saving rates. Corporate saving rates languished between 1½ and 2½ percent of GDP from 1970–90, and then rose modestly in the 1990s. It was only in the early 2000s that corporate saving rose much more sharply, from 4.5 percent in 2003 to a peak of 9.5 percent prior to the global financial crisis. This occurred primarily due to significant restructuring of corporate balance sheets in the early 2000s.

ARE INDIA'S IMBALANCES A PROBLEM?

Large fiscal imbalances pose risks to macroeconomic stability and domestic growth objectives, perpetuate financial restrictions that create distortions, and restrain development of the financial sector. The primary effects of fiscal imbalances fall on India itself, although a collapse in the country's growth would slow the global economy, and a sudden stop in capital inflows could create financial disruptions for other economies. Key problem areas are examined below.

Financial Sector and Growth Implications

The perpetuation of financial sector investment restrictions will likely pose a significant constraint on India's ability to realize its development potential. Subjecting domestic financial institutions (banks, insurance, and provident funds) to punitive regulatory requirements, and distorting credit markets by setting deposit rates that do not necessarily reflect market conditions, distorts the allocation of private saving, crowds out private investment, and potentially lowers growth.[16]

Financial restrictions on asset purchases, for example, limit financial deepening and restrain much-needed infrastructure investment. Mandated purchase of government securities has curtailed the availability of domestic credit for the private sector and restrained development of a corporate bond market. Although

---

[16]The positive effects on growth from unwinding investment restrictions could potentially involve some trade-offs. In particular, such unwinding could affect fiscal dynamics by raising the growth-adjusted effective interest rate paid on government debt.

caps on foreign purchases of domestic bonds have been raised substantially in recent years, foreign participation has not increased significantly—held back by other impediments such as minimum maturity requirements, unfavorable tax treatment, and lock-in periods.

Meanwhile, firms have been forced to borrow from commercial banks at adjustable rates, or borrow long term in foreign currency, to fund investment projects, which has raised exposure to currency and interest rate risk. Given segmentation in credit markets, credit constraints have been particularly acute for SMEs. Aside from the usual crowding out of private investment due to large public dissaving, policy-induced distortions in lending and borrowing rates have also served to reduce credit for the private sector. Capital controls, instituted with a view toward minimizing exchange rate risk and preserving macroeconomic stability, have hindered firms' access to foreign saving at competitive prices. If capital account restrictions were gradually eased, there could be further efficiency gains in financial intermediation and greater availability of credit for domestic entities.[17]

With large infrastructure needs and limited fiscal space, India's Eleventh Five-Year Plan (2007–12) called for higher private sector involvement in much-needed infrastructure investment. The long-term nature of these projects has, however, laid bare the impediments to meeting these goals. A particular concern for the bank-dominated financial system is the risk of large maturity mismatches, while capital controls have limited foreign financing. Coupled with deep structural rigidities, including governance problems and implementation risks, envisaged private sector participation in this critical sphere of development could again fall short of targets.

Macroeconomic Stability Implications

Fiscal consolidation should help maintain macroeconomic stability, create policy space for contingent needs, and limit vulnerability to external shocks. As evident from recent developments in major advanced economies, market sentiment toward sovereigns with large fiscal imbalances can shift abruptly, resulting in higher risk premiums and adverse debt dynamics. The following are the key elements of fiscal consolidation:

- *Narrowing of the growth-interest differential.* Public debt has grown even as growth-interest differentials have been large and positive. In part, this is because a number of factors have kept the cost of government borrowing low, including the captive base for government securities and capital

---

[17]Since the 1990s, capital controls have been gradually liberalized, and remaining restrictions are focused on areas such as foreign purchases of Indian bonds and resident outflows. The full removal of capital controls must, however, be mindful of the risks involved, including a possible increase in domestic interest rates (if Indian financial intermediaries decide to move assets abroad), as well as higher volatility of interest rates, which could be damaging for growth. Furthermore, as capital controls strengthened India's resilience to potentially destabilizing outflows during the recent crisis, authorities must retain sufficient flexibility to put them in place if circumstances dictate doing so.

controls. But the large differential is unlikely to persist, especially if integration with global financial markets continues to increase and SLR requirements on domestic financial institutions ease. Independently, a protracted growth shock could set public debt on a potentially unstable path.

- *Reconstituting fiscal space.* A perpetuation of fiscal imbalances limits the space for countercyclical policies when needed, and raises the risk of a higher risk premium on debt over the medium term. Interest payments currently absorb 25 percent of total revenues, and could become explosive if yields were to rise.

- *External balance.* Higher public and private sector investment, notably in infrastructure projects, and lower private saving (to the extent that household saving reflects the lack of social insurance) are both desirable. To minimize pressure on the current account, these shifts in national investment and private saving must be offset by smaller government budget deficits.

HOW TO ADDRESS IMBALANCES

To address imbalances and sustain high growth, India should embark on durable fiscal consolidation, while increasing public investment in much-needed infrastructure projects. The plan to bring the general government deficit down by 2015, anchored by a broad-based consumption tax, is an appropriate objective. The key will be implementation. Relaxing investment restrictions on financial institutions would create a favorable environment for increasing private sector participation in infrastructure development. To the extent that high private saving reflects the lack of social insurance, safety nets could be strengthened. The key domestic policy priorities are elaborated in turn below.

Tax Reforms

Given the projected and necessary increase in public infrastructure investment, and pressing social needs, tax reforms are critical for fiscal adjustment. Overperformance of public finances during the current expansion will help reconstitute fiscal space. Although revenue growth has been relatively strong in the recovery, there is further scope to widen the tax base, streamline collection, and improve compliance. A key challenge of current tax proposals is to overcome the political economy of shifting tax collections from the center to the state, given the increasing relative power of the states.

A nationwide Goods and Services Tax (GST) would simplify the tax system, widen the tax base, and increase revenues in the long run. The government has recommended implementing a GST as a value-added tax.[18] This tax would replace

---

[18]The proposal is that the central government would tax goods at 10 percent, services at 8 percent, and essentials at 6 percent, with the recommendation that states add identical rates. That is, the total rate on goods would be 20 percent.

India's web of state- and national-level excise, sales, and value-added taxes with a unified consumption-tax framework, and draw in the entire consumption base by taxing imports while excluding exports. Although this reform has been designed to be revenue-neutral, the replacement of India's current system with the more streamlined GST is likely to raise compliance and hence revenues.

Reform of the personal and corporate income tax code is long overdue. The scope of the government's proposal for a new Direct Tax Code (DTC), which has provisions to limit deductions and widen the tax base, could be expanded. Although the DTC is planned as revenue-neutral, implementation of it in combination with the GST will likely enhance growth by reducing distortions.

Improving tax compliance and enforcement could significantly raise tax revenues. That less than 5 percent of the population pays income tax even as the ranks of the middle class have swelled is indicative of room to raise income tax revenues by increasing compliance. Accelerating the development of a National Population Register, thus far discussed in the context of better targeting subsidies to the poor (see below), could vastly improve tax collections.

Finally, more ambitious revenue-raising reforms should also be considered. For example, rates on the top income brackets (currently 30.9 percent) could be increased, possibly by reversing the recent reduction of the highest income tax bracket. Given the scope for tax arbitrage if personal income tax rates are raised and corporate tax rates are reduced, any reform of the tax code must take into account the full impact of a tax revision on raising revenue.

Spending Reforms

Greater spending efficiency of government programs is key to square the stated consolidation objectives with significant social and infrastructure needs. Policy priorities are to shift government funds from nonessential expenditure toward infrastructure development, better allocate funds for subsidies, improve targeting, and increase the use of performance-based incentives to improve spending efficiency. Other reforms, such as land reform and reducing red tape, would improve governance and policy predictability but are also critical for infrastructure development.

There is significant potential for reforms of subsidies to reduce costs and improve social outcomes. Major subsidies, notably on fuel products, impose a high cost on the government budget, are poorly targeted (and mostly regressive), and present opportunities for arbitrage. Recent subsidy reforms, including liberalization of petrol prices, are a step in the right direction. Additional reforms include replacement of some subsidies with targeted support (e.g., cash vouchers) and accelerating development of the National Population Register and Unique Identification Number (UID) to help target subsidies more effectively.

The planned expansion of social spending must be undertaken with a view toward increased efficiency of implementation. Given the country's pressing social needs, expanding education and employment programs are necessary to achieve inclusive growth. Furthermore, steps could be taken to ensure that the food security bill currently being discussed, which proposes to provide subsidized rice or wheat to eligible households, is affordable and well-targeted. To reconcile expansion of social programs with planned fiscal consolidation, it is critical to improve spending efficiency (e.g., by making greater use of performance-based incentives). Without such efficiency gains, targets in the FRBMA could only be met by tightly constraining public investment, which would undermine growth.

The commitment to fiscal consolidation in the 2011/12 budget as well as in the Government Debt Report has improved transparency and strengthened India's medium-term budget framework. Authorities could also provide details quantifying how they envisage fitting rising capital and social expenditures into a budget envelope that declines as a share of GDP. To minimize the risk of reversals in consolidation, it is crucial to amend the FRBMA, as recommended by the Thirteenth Finance Commission, including by tightening escape clauses and introducing a fiscal oversight committee.

Financial Sector Reforms

Ensuring more efficient intermediation of domestic savings will require a concerted effort toward financial sector reform. Gradually reducing the SLR will not only free up funds for private borrowing but will also allow government bond interest rates to become truly market-determined. That would allow government rates to become true benchmarks, paving the way for the development of the corporate bond market. At the same time, steps should be taken to boost bond market liquidity and develop securitization and hedging instruments both to ensure sufficient long-term rupee debt resources for domestic investment needs, and to help banks manage their liquidity and concentration risks.[19] Meanwhile, continued reduction of the SLR and opening of the financial sector would provide government the incentive to adjust by narrowing its base of captive finance.

Development of a health insurance industry will aid in reducing households' precautionary saving. Studies indicate that the financial burden on Indian households from health spending is significant (Balarajan, Selvaraj, and Subramanian, 2011). Over 70 percent of all health spending is out of pocket (USAID, 2008), and the 2004 National Sample Survey revealed that about 6 percent of families became impoverished due to health expenses. A slowly growing private health care industry is largely unregulated and costly for most, and only 20 percent of the population has any form of health insurance. Steps must be taken to expand hospitalization insurance, including through partnerships between the government and nongovernmental organizations, in order to improve access to health care, minimize out-of-pocket expenses, and reduce the precautionary basis for household saving.

---

[19]Steps taken to reduce statutory requirements on the purchase of government securities must be mindful that banks continue to abide by international best practice (i.e., Basel liquidity standards).

TOWARD GLOBAL ACTION

Strengthened policy actions in India should consider fiscal consolidation along with the removal of distortive financial restrictions as part of global rebalancing efforts across major economies. Fiscal adjustment—improving the government's budget deficit after five years—would be in accordance with the Thirteenth Finance Commission's medium-term plans. Fiscal adjustment should rely primarily on revenue-raising measures. Reduced SLR requirements on banks would free resources for the private sector, reducing their real cost of capital and thereby boosting investment. For the government, liberalizing financial controls would entail higher interest rates (larger debt service), which would be offset by higher value-added tax and labor income tax revenues. Specific reforms would include an increase in the consumption tax (GST), which would minimize tax distortions and which at present is very low by international comparison, as well as an increase in labor income taxes. Raising the GST may not suffice to reduce the budget deficit to target levels, in which case remaining revenues would come from the increase in labor income taxes.

REFERENCES

Balarajan, Y., S. Selvaraj, and S.V. Subramanian, 2011, "Health Care and Equity in India," *Lancet*, Vol. 377, No. 9764, pp. 505–15.

Banerjee, A., and E. Duflo, 2002, "Do Firms Want to Borrow More? Testing Credit Constraints Using a Directed Lending Program," MIT Working Paper No. 02-25.

Comptroller and Auditor General of India, 2008, *Union Audit Reports: Performance Audit Report No. 11 of 2008* (New Delhi: Comptroller and Auditor General of India).

International Monetary Fund (IMF), 2010, "India—Staff Report for the 2010 Article IV Consultation" (Washington: International Monetary Fund).

———, 2012, "India—Staff Report for the 2012 Article IV Consultation" (Washington: International Monetary Fund).

Piketty, T., and N. Qian, 2009, "Income Inequality and Progressive Income Taxation in China and India, 1986-2015" *American Economic Journal,* Vol. 1, No. 2, pp. 53–63.

Singh, N., and T.N. Srinivasan, 2005, "Fiscal Policy in India: Lessons and Priorities," Santa Cruz Center for International Economics Working Paper No. 555 (Santa Cruz: University of California).

U.S. Agency for International Development (USAID), 2008, "Private Health Insurance in India: Promise and Reality," report prepared by BearingPoint, Inc. for USAID, February (Washington: USAID). http://transition.usaid.gov/in/our_work/pdfs/promise_reality.pdf.

PART III

Imbalances in Major Surplus Economies

CHAPTER 7

China: Imbalances and High Saving

SHAUN K. ROACHE[1]

China's rapid growth has been accompanied by large external surpluses, reflecting an exceptionally high level of national saving. Behind this high saving lie a number of distortions that have reduced welfare both in China and the rest of the world. To address this problem, policies will need to bolster social insurance, increase exchange rate flexibility, and liberalize domestic interest rates.

China has followed an unusual development path, combining exceptionally rapid growth with large external surpluses. Most other countries in the early stages of an economic take-off have run current account deficits, drawing on foreign saving to fund domestic investment opportunities. But China has been different: it has run a current account surplus persistently for the past two decades. For some time, the surplus remained quite stable and modest, but in 2003 it suddenly began to surge, reaching 10 percent of GDP by 2007. A rising trade surplus accounted for over three-quarters of the rising current account balance, with the remainder largely due to a higher income surplus.[2] After that, the current account surplus receded to about 3 percent of GDP in 2011. Still, it remains above its 1990s levels and significantly above the G20 average (Figure 7.1).

The large current account surpluses reflect exceptionally high rates of saving. National saving as a percent of GDP has been rising steadily for the past two decades. Nearly half of the total has traditionally come from the household sector, but the contribution of corporate saving has increased very rapidly and is now almost equally large, while public saving has also made a significant contribution (Figure 7.2). Saving by all three sectors as a percent of GDP is now among the highest in the G20 (excluding oil exporters). As a result, the overall national saving rate stood at about 51 percent of GDP in 2011, more than double the average for the other G20 countries (excluding oil exporters).

The rise in household saving as a percent of GDP has been particularly striking, because household incomes have actually been falling relative to GDP

---

[1]Shaun K. Roache is a Senior Economist in the IMF Western Hemisphere Department. This chapter was written with guidance from Josh Felman and support from Eric Bang, David Reichsfeld, and Anne Lalramnghakhleli Moses.
[2]This reflects, in part, rising net interest income receipts from accumulating net foreign assets comprised mainly of foreign exchange reserves.

Figure 7.1 China: Current Account Balance *(Percent of GDP)*

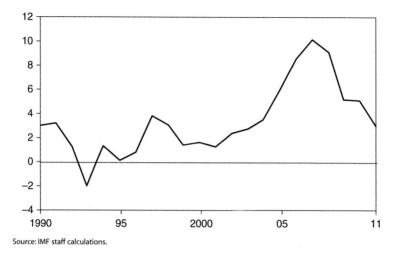

Source: IMF staff calculations.

Figure 7.2 China: Saving by Sector *(Percent of GDP)*

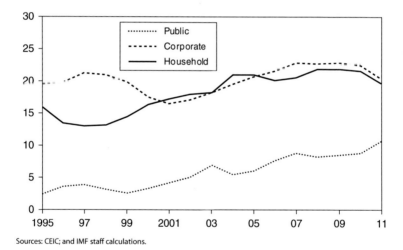

Sources: CEIC; and IMF staff calculations.

(Figure 7.3). Employment growth has been disappointing relative to the pace of economic growth, while rural wages and business incomes have stagnated, and capital income has been hit by a sharp decline in real deposit rates. These factors have more than offset a rapid rise in wages in the modern manufacturing sector.[3]

---

[3]The link between labor compensation in urban and rural areas is weakened by the household registration system, which impedes labor mobility and sustains wage gaps, even after accounting for differences in productivity. As a result, the disparities between rural and urban incomes, as well as health and education outcomes, have widened significantly in recent years. See Meng and Zhang (2001).

Figure 7.3 China: Household Saving Rate *(Percent)*

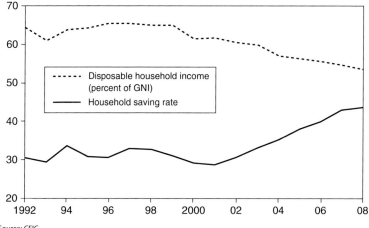

Source: CEIC.
Note: GNI = gross national income.

Figure 7.4 China: Saving and Investment *(Percent of GDP)*

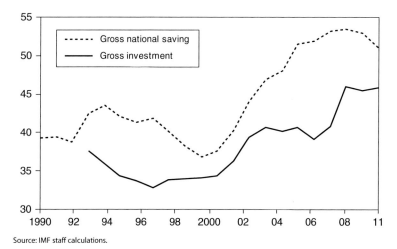

Source: IMF staff calculations.

Accordingly, the rate of household saving has soared to extraordinary heights when measured relative to disposable income. As household saving has risen, the consumption share has fallen to less than one-third of GDP.

The rise in saving has been accompanied by a similar—but less pronounced—increase in the investment rate (Figure 7.4). In fact, China's growth model has been remarkably capital-intensive, notwithstanding the abundance of labor. The capital stock has grown at an estimated 12 percent annual rate since 2000, far exceeding employment growth, which has averaged less than 1 percent per year.

From a demand perspective, investment—not net exports—has been the primary contributor to the country's 10 percent average growth over the past two

Figure 7.5 China: Contributions to Growth *(Percent)*

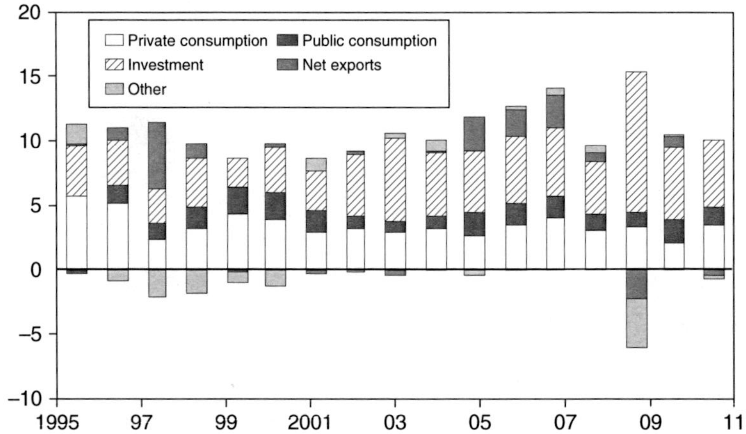

Source: IMF staff calculations.

decades. The surge of investment has taken place in two waves, the first coming in the early 2000s as the country built up its heavy industries (such as steel, machinery, and chemicals) and the second following the global financial crisis, as the government's stimulus package set off a large construction boom (Figure 7.5). Following these surges, investment in 2011 reached 46 percent of GDP, higher than in any other G20 country.[4] Even so, it remains well below the level of national saving.

China's model of growth has lifted a remarkable number of people out of poverty. Between 1981 and 2004, the proportion of China's population below the World Bank's defined poverty line fell from 65 percent to 10 percent, a decline of over half a billion people (World Bank, 2009). A fall in the number of poor of this magnitude over such a short period is without historical precedent.

Both the Chinese authorities and IMF staff expect that the surges in saving and investment will come to an end over the medium term. The prospects for the current account depend on whether saving slows more than investment. The following developments are envisaged:

- The current investment boom is expected to fade as macroeconomic stimulus wanes and private investment in housing and manufacturing returns to a more normal level.

- The Chinese authorities anticipate that their planned policies will reduce saving. In particular, the wide-ranging reform agenda set out in the Twelfth Five-Year Plan aims to rebalance the economy in favor of consumption (Box 7.1). Accordingly, the authorities expect that saving will decelerate at

---

[4]Based on IMF staff estimates for 2011 in the April 2012 *World Economic Outlook* (IMF, 2012) and excluding inventory accumulation.

BOX 7.1

How China's Twelfth Five-Year Plan Targets a Rebalanced Economy

China's Twelfth Five-Year Plan covering the period from 2011–16 sets out an ambitious reform agenda that, if implemented in a timely manner and sequenced appropriately, would move the economy much further toward a balanced growth path. The agenda includes the following initiatives:

- *Expanding domestic consumption* through stronger social safety nets (including health and retirement programs), an increased supply of health services, and economic growth that is more labor-intensive and can raise the growth rate of wage incomes, particularly for the lowest-paid (including raising the minimum wage).
- *Rebalancing the sectoral structure.* One notable target is to raise the service sector's contribution by 4 percentage points of GDP to 47 percent, in part by liberalizing markets (including reducing barriers to entry), equalizing factor costs (including power, water, and heating) with the industrial sector, and improving the managed floating exchange rate regime based on market supply and demand. Enhanced environmental protection and safety may also moderate investment growth in heavy industry.
- *Further liberalizing the financial sector and improving access.* Plans include market-based reform of interest rates, increasing capital account openness, and strengthening rural financial institutions to boost access to credit and other financial services.

about the same pace as investment, so the current account surpluses would remain below 5 percent of GDP. As for the exchange rate, the authorities emphasize progress made in increasing its flexibility, while noting the generally weak relationship between exchange rate movements and the current account.

- IMF staff also expect saving to fall, albeit modestly. While the Twelfth Five-Year Plan holds out considerable potential to change this situation, it may take some time before a critical mass of measures is in place, and further time before the effects are felt. IMF staff expect the current account surplus to remain somewhat below 5 percent of GDP (IMF, 2011b), but moderating investment should offset modestly declining saving to cause the current account to drift higher from current levels over the medium term. (This projection assumes that the real effective exchange rate is maintained at current levels.) In other words, without additional and prompt action, imbalances will be lower than peak 2007 levels but will remain significant, with both saving and investment remaining very high.

ROOT CAUSES OF IMBALANCES

China's imbalances are rooted deep in the economy's structure. They can be traced to the signature measure of the 1990s—the reform of state-owned enterprises (SOEs)—that paved the way for rising saving and external surpluses. Subsequent policies, together with distortions that have built up over the years, have resulted in an economic framework that has sustained high saving and exacerbated external imbalances.

By the 1990s, a reform of the SOEs was much needed. In previous decades, agriculture had been liberalized and private enterprise allowed to flourish. But the manufacturing sector remained dominated by large state firms, which were absorbing the bulk of the country's saving yet were producing little economic return. In response, the government enacted a sweeping set of measures aimed at improving SOE efficiency and profitability. Most notably, enterprises were relieved of their obligation to provide social services (such as medical insurance and pensions) to their employees and were instructed to operate instead on a commercial basis. In addition, many enterprises benefited from capital injections and debt reductions.

The reform proved remarkably successful. The newly unshackled SOEs improved their efficiency significantly, becoming internationally competitive in many cases, particularly in heavy industries. This triggered an investment boom, which has led to a significant increase in China's industrial capacity—that is, the size of its tradable goods sector.

At the same time, however, the subsequent evolution of policies produced the imbalances that characterize the economy today. In effect, the SOE reform transferred resources from the household sector (and the government) to firms. In and of itself, this was hardly decisive. As the SOEs improved their productivity, the returns would normally have flowed back to households and the government, thereby restoring the distribution of income and minimizing any consequences for imbalances. But this did not happen. Instead, the imbalances only grew larger, reflecting a complex variety of factors. In part, the evolving growth model brought to the fore some existing distortions (such as the failure of SOEs to pay dividends) and in part it created new ones (such as the lack of a social safety net). Also important was the government reaction (such as its foreign exchange policy). All of these factors acted to preserve and even intensify the imbalances.

Corporate Saving

The high levels of corporate saving in China are partly the product of market forces, but more importantly the result of sizable distortions to the prices of factor inputs, product market competition, and dividend policy. SOE reforms initially produced a sharp rise in corporate saving. As firms improved their efficiency and expanded their operations, profits soared and investment followed. In most cases, the increase in capital intensity would have eventually driven down rates of return, causing profitability to subside. Remarkably, the opposite has occurred: the corporate saving rate has continued to increase for nearly two decades (though at a diminished pace since 2005) (Figure 7.6).

Several factors explain why, including some related to market forces at work in the economy. For example, the composition of the economy has been changing, as the SOEs that have encountered diminishing returns have been giving way to

Figure 7.6 China: Corporate Saving and Investment *(Percent of GDP)*

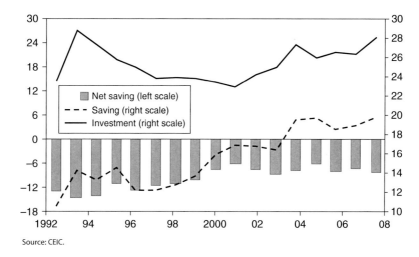

Source: CEIC.

an even more efficient private sector. Over the past few decades, the locus of global manufacturing activity has shifted to China, as the country has become the "workshop of the world." This shift has boosted profits not only in China but in companies throughout the world, as both sides have benefited from the specialization allowed by international trade.

Another factor sustaining profitability may be the abundant supply of labor. The large reservoir of poorly-paid rural workers may have depressed manufacturing wages, preventing them from rising in line with productivity, and allowing firms to capture the benefits as profits. This may be a key reason why the labor share of income has fallen. Official data on the manufacturing sector, however, show that wages have risen rapidly, essentially in line with productivity.

Other factors directly related to policy distortions are:

- *Subsidized factor input prices.* Factor inputs, such as land, water, energy, and capital, have increasingly been subsidized in recent years, effectively transferring growing amounts of public resources to the corporate sector. Studies estimate the total value of China's factor market distortions has now reached almost 10 percent of GDP.[5]

- *The market power of SOEs.* Profits in key sectors have not been competed away by other firms, because the policy framework has encouraged large SOE "national champions" that enjoy significant domestic market power (Song, Storesletten, and Zilibotti, 2011; Tyers and Lu, 2008).

- *Dividend policy.* The increase in profits has largely been saved, since SOEs have had no incentive to pay dividends, nor have they really been forced to

---

[5]See the People's Republic of China Article IV Staff Report (IMF, 2010) and the People's Republic of China Spillover Report (IMF, 2011a).

Figure 7.7 G20: Saving and Current Accounts *(Percent of GDP, average from 2001–10)*

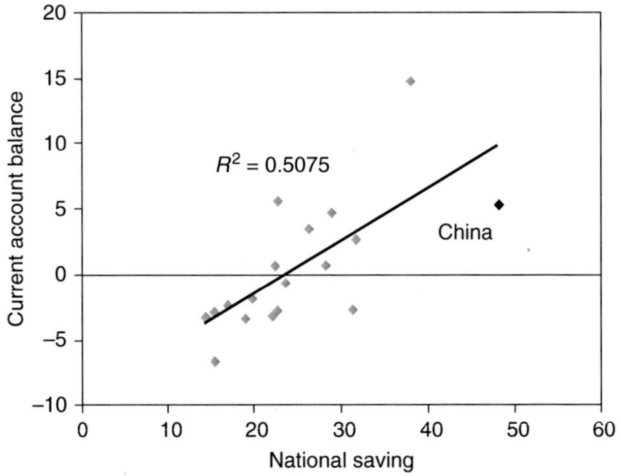

Source: IMF staff calculations.

do so. (In some cases, dividends have been paid out to state administrators, which have then recycled them back to the firms.)

But all this raises a question: if these distortions have boosted profits, why haven't they had a similarly powerful effect on investment?[6] In countries where capital controls allow interest rates to be determined domestically, higher saving normally reduces interest rates and spurs investment. China's real interest rates have declined, but the rise in investment, until recently, has been smaller than the rise in saving. The likely reason is that as the level of investment increases, implementation costs (managerial and otherwise) rise even more rapidly, putting a brake on this activity. And China's rate of investment is remarkably high—at 45 percent of GDP, it is the highest in the G20 by far—implying that the "adjustment costs" (i.e., of further increases in investment) are exceptionally high (Figure 7.7).[7] Accordingly, countries with unusually high levels of gross national saving tend to have positive *net* saving; i.e., current account surpluses.

Household Saving

Household saving in China has been affected by three key distortions—large gaps in the social safety net, credit rationing, and interest rate distortions, as well as to a lesser extent by the household registration system that impedes the movement of labor.

---

[6]See Ferri and Liu (2010) and Huang and Tao (2010).

[7]For this reason, investment is quite insensitive to the marginal value of additional capital (represented by Tobin's Q, the ratio of the market value of an asset to its replacement cost). For example, estimates of the elasticity of investment to Q often range between 0.01 and 0.05.

The 1990s SOE reform affected household saving in two key ways. First, it dismantled social safety nets. The removal of SOEs' social obligations shifted much of the burden of providing for sickness and old age onto households. They responded by increasing their precautionary saving, a phenomenon that has only intensified in recent years as the population has begun to age.

The second way the SOE reform affected household saving was through housing privatization. The privatization of the housing stock has led younger households to increase their saving to accumulate the funds required to purchase property. A growing population of young workers must now save for the substantial down payments required for a property purchase.[8] As the economy has boomed and housing prices have increased, saving requirements have grown commensurately.

These two changes in turn interacted with distortions from financial sector restrictions and controls, particularly credit rationing and interest rate distortions, and the household registration system.

With interest rates held below market levels, loan demand has long been high and banks have been forced to ration credit. In these circumstances, banks have preferred to lend to SOEs that benefit from implicit state guarantees. Accordingly, saving has been the only way for most households to insure against risks, smooth their consumption in the event of unanticipated expenditures, or purchase housing.[9] Rationing has also forced smaller businesses to self-fund investment projects. At the same time, low real interest rates reflecting controls have reduced household deposit income (see Lardy, 2008, and the following section).

Finally, labor income itself has been held back, in part because the household registration system has fragmented the labor market, so that demand for labor in the fast-growing coastal provinces has had only limited effects on wages inland. Empirical research has found significant evidence that rural migrants are segregated from their urban counterparts in terms of job opportunities and wages, although labor market competition between the two groups is increasing (Knight and Yueh, 2009; Wu, 2005).

In recent years, China has been repairing the social safety net, but more still needs to be done. Significant resources have been allocated to improving the pension, health care, and education systems. A new rural pension scheme has been launched, pension benefits have been made portable, and subsidies for health insurance have been increased. But gross social transfers are still well below international comparators, and large gaps in the net consequently remain. For example, the health system still creates a strong incentive for precautionary saving because out-of-pocket expenses are high and coverage for catastrophic illnesses is limited.

---

[8]The increasing number of households and rising demand for upgraded property relative to the supply of pre-SOE-reform housing stock that may be bequeathed mean that privatization should increase aggregate household saving.

[9]Though mortgages have become increasingly common in recent years.

Policy Response: Adapting to High Saving

The government has reacted to rising saving by encouraging exports, so that aggregate demand will be sufficient to sustain output close to potential. To do this, the government has intervened on the foreign exchange market and accumulated reserves, thereby keeping the exchange rate at a low (i.e., depreciated) level. In effect, this approach has allowed the economy to adapt to high levels of saving. Moreover, the way in which this intervention has been sterilized has transferred income to the government, reinforcing domestic saving and thereby sustaining the imbalances.

As higher saving has pushed up the current account balance, the authorities have reacted in a variety of ways, including the following:

- *Exchange rate appreciation.* To a certain extent, the exchange rate has been allowed to appreciate. The average real effective exchange rate (REER) for the 12 months through mid-2012 was about 18 percent higher than the average for the previous two decades (Figure 7.8). This is a significant amount. But it falls far short of what might be expected, given the evolution of China's economy over this period, particularly its productivity gains relative to trading partners (Figure 7.9). One possible explanation is that the real exchange rate has had to remain low so that weak domestic demand could be offset by high external demand, thereby keeping aggregate output close to potential. According to IMF staff estimates (IMF, 2011b), this leaves the REER moderately below the level consistent with medium-term fundamentals.

- *Massive sterilization.* China has responded to the large current account surpluses by purchasing foreign exchange and sterilizing the proceeds. As a

Figure 7.8 China: Reserves and the Exchange Rate

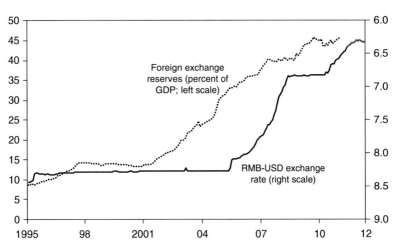

Source: Thomson Datastream.

Figure 7.9 China: Relative Productivity and the Real Exchange Rate *(Log change multiplied by 100 from 1990)*

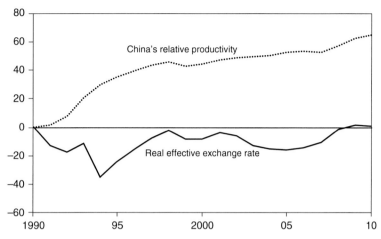

Source: IMF staff calculations.
Note: Relative productivity of tradable sector versus nontradable sector in China (relative to trading partners).

Figure 7.10 China: Change in Cumulative Reserves *(January–June cumulative; in billions of U.S. dollars)*

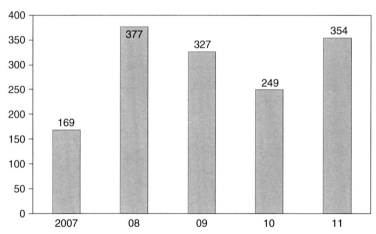

Source: Thomson Datastream.

result, reserves now exceed $3 trillion, nearly half of GDP, while sterilization instruments account for almost the same amount (Figure 7.10). Since reserves began rising sharply in 2001, the required reserve ratio on domestic renminbi deposits has been ratcheted higher on more than 30 occasions to reach its current 20 percent. The central bank has also issued a large quantity of short-term bills.

Figure 7.11   China: Real Interest Rates *(Percent)*

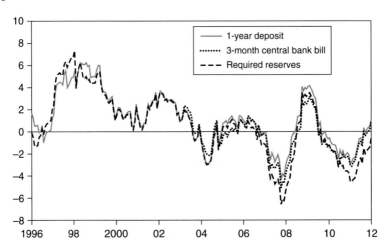

Source: Thomson Datastream.

- *Distorted interest rates.* This sterilization has been achieved at below-market interest rates. Key interest rates declined in real terms after the surpluses started to accelerate in the early 2000s (Figure 7.11). In fact, real rates on required reserves (the key sterilization instrument), central bank bills, and deposits have been very low for most of the subsequent period and negative when the current account surplus was at its peak. Savers have been unable to respond by shifting funds abroad, because of extensive capital controls.

- *Implicit transfers from households to government.* As a result, sterilization has resulted in a large transfer from households (depositors) to the government (borrowers).[10] Since 2003, annual household interest earnings have been as much as 4 percentage points of GDP lower than if real interest rates had been maintained at their 1998–2002 average (Figure 7.12).[11]

- *Increased national saving.* This process of sterilization-and-transfer reinforced the current account surplus in the period leading up to 2008, because the government effectively saved funds that might have been consumed, thereby adding to national saving. The process was only reversed in the wake of the global financial crisis, when the government decided to shift its fiscal stance and stimulate the economy.

---

[10]Corporations have benefited much less because they have large deposits as well as loans, a reflection of their high saving rate.

[11]Note that the peak transfers occurred in 2008, close to when the current account surplus reached its peak (2007).

Figure 7.12 China: Personal Saving One-Year Deposit Interest Rates *(Nominal percent per annum)*

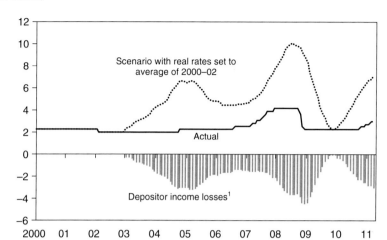

Sources: CEIC; Thomson Datastream; and IMF staff calculations.
[1]Annualized household interest income loss in percent of GDP for scenario with real interest rates at 1998–2002 average compared to actual deposit interest rates. Nominal rate calculated as the real rate plus the two-year trailing average inflation rate.

In summary, key elements of the policy response have actually helped sustain the imbalances.

ARE CHINA'S IMBALANCES A PROBLEM?

China's growth model has been based on high domestic saving, counterbalanced by high external demand and equilibrated by a low real exchange rate. In many respects, it has been remarkably successful, delivering rapid growth and lifting hundreds of millions of people out of poverty. But as the Chinese authorities recognize, the model ultimately needs to change.

The removal of key distortions would bring two critical benefits to China: higher household consumption and enhanced macroeconomic control.

First, rebalancing could re-equilibrate the distribution of income back toward households, allowing them to raise their consumption share from its current low level (as a percent of GDP), which is less than half the level in most other G20 countries. Rebalancing could also address rising inequality between rural and urban households, since it is the former that particularly lack social insurance, access to credit and other financial services, and the ability to supply their labor to fast-growing industries.

Second, rebalancing could enable the monetary policy framework to move away from quantitative controls (which have the side-effect of shifting transactions away from the regulated banking system) toward a market-based framework that can aim more efficiently at inflation and financial stability targets. It would also allow broader financial sector reforms that would end credit rationing and improve the allocation of the nation's saving.

HOW TO ADDRESS IMBALANCES

To rebalance its economy, China needs to address the underlying structural factors that contribute to its high saving and current account surpluses. Most of the needed measures are already contained in the Twelfth Five-Year Plan. But success will depend on their implementation, and in some cases (such as the exchange rate), more needs to be done.

Policy Priorities

Steps are needed to further strengthen social safety nets. Recent analysis by IMF staff indicates that higher government social spending allows households to reduce their precautionary saving, with important income, insurance, and distributional (and welfare) effects (Baldacci and others, 2010; Barnett and Brooks, 2010). In particular, a sustained 1 percentage point of GDP increase in government social spending would allow households to increase their consumption ratio by up to 1¼ percentage points of GDP. Accordingly, China should continue to improve access to high-quality health care, reduce out-of-pocket expenses, and bolster coverage for catastrophic illness. It would also be important to consolidate the complex and fragmented patchwork of various national, provincial, and occupational pension schemes for migrant and rural workers.

Increased exchange rate flexibility would be an integral component of rebalancing. Boosting domestic consumption, including through social safety net reforms, would increase domestic demand. To avoid overheating, and a possibly disruptive real exchange rate appreciation through higher domestic inflation, the nominal exchange rate should be allowed to appreciate on a multilateral basis (that is, in nominal effective terms). This would also change firms' incentives, encouraging them to rebalance their investment away from the export-focused tradable sector and toward the domestic service sector. Moreover, by allowing the exchange rate to absorb more of the ongoing appreciation pressures, it would also reduce the need for sterilization. Interest rates could then be allowed to rise to market levels, reducing the implicit tax on households and allowing them to raise their consumption.[12]

Further efforts are needed to liberalize and develop the financial system. This would provide households and firms with a broader range of financing possibilities, again allowing them to increase their consumption and investment. Recent IMF staff estimates suggest that financial sector reform, together with an appreciated real exchange rate and more developed capital markets, would have a significant impact on external imbalances (Geng and N'Diaye, 2012). For example, the expansion of nonbank financial intermediation, including a well-functioning bond market, could facilitate growth in private pensions and insurance, reducing the need for households to save (and effectively help the government expand the safety net).

---

[12]See the China 2011 Article IV Staff Report (IMF, 2011b).

Distributions from the profits of SOEs should be increased. Majority state-owned and publically listed Chinese enterprises pay dividends to stockholders but have not distributed significant amounts to the government. Raising the current payout rate of zero to 15 percent (as announced in 2007 but not yet implemented) would bring China closer into line with international comparators and reduce gross corporate saving. If the proceeds are, in turn, consumed by the government or transferred to households, this would boost aggregate consumption.

Labor mobility can be improved by liberalizing the household registration system. This would ease labor market constraints in fast-growing regions and spur more labor-intensive growth in these parts of the country. At the same time, it would improve incomes in rural areas, thereby helping to narrow wide rural-urban income inequalities.

Removing factor cost distortions and allowing greater competition in domestic markets would improve resource allocation. The costs of major factor inputs such as land, energy, and water need to be raised to market levels to ensure more efficient allocation of resources and more appropriate pricing of externalities. Steps should also be taken to reduce barriers to entry. Both steps would help scale back the corporate saving that arises from redistribution, rather than competition and market forces.

TOWARD GLOBAL ACTION

A reduction in China's imbalances would benefit the global economy. Typically, the rest of the world would respond to an increase in saving by a large country such as China by reducing interest rates, as discussed in Chapter 2 of this volume. This would have the advantage of bolstering domestic demand in China's trading partners, thereby maintaining output at potential. But in the current circumstances advanced countries do not have this option: their interest rates are already so low they could not reduce them even if desired global saving were to increase. In other words, they are in a liquidity trap, as discussed earlier. In this case, large current account surpluses in some countries can lead to low aggregate demand and lower output in other countries.[13] Conversely, if China were able to rebalance its economy toward domestic demand, this could increase global output.

REFERENCES

Baldacci, Emanuele, Giovanni Callegari, David Coady, Ding Ding, Manmohan Kumar, Pietro Tommasino, and Jaejoon Woo, 2010, "Public Expenditures on Social Programs and Household Consumption in China," IMF Working Paper 10/69 (Washington: International Monetary Fund).

---

[13]In principle, these countries could use fiscal policy to sustain domestic demand, but under current circumstances the room for fiscal policy is severely curtailed by debt sustainability concerns.

Barnett, Steven, and Ray Brooks, 2010, "China: Does Government Health and Education Spending Boost Consumption?" IMF Working Paper 10/16 (Washington: International Monetary Fund).

Ferri, Giovanni, and Li-Gang Liu, 2010, "Honor Thy Creditors Before Thy Shareholders: Are the Profits of Chinese State-Owned Enterprises Real?" *Asian Economic Papers*, Vol. 9, No. 3, pp. 50–71.

Geng, Nan, and Papa N'Diaye, 2012, "Determinants of Corporate Investment in China: Evidence from Cross-Country Firm Level Data," IMF Working Paper 12/80 (Washington: International Monetary Fund).

Huang, Yiping, and Kunyu Tao, 2010, "Causes and Remedies of China's External Imbalances," China Center for Economic Research Working Paper 2010–02.

International Monetary Fund (IMF), 2010, "People's Republic of China—Staff Report for the 2010 Article IV Consultation," SM/10/191, July (Washington: International Monetary Fund).

———, 2011a, "People's Republic of China—Spillover Report—2011 Article IV Consultation," July (Washington: International Monetary Fund).

———, 2011b, "People's Republic of China—Staff Report for the 2011 Article IV Consultation," July (Washington: International Monetary Fund).

———, 2012, *World Economic Outlook: Growth Resuming, Dangers Remain*, April (Washington: International Monetary Fund).

Knight, John, and Linda Yueh, 2009, "Segmentation or Competition in China's Urban Labour Market?" *Cambridge Journal of Economics*, Vol. 33, No. 1, pp. 79–94.

Lardy, Nicholas R., 2008, "Financial Repression in China," Peterson Institute Policy Brief PB08–8 (Washington: Peterson Institute for International Economics).

Meng, Xin, and Junsen Zhang, 2001, "The Two-Tier Labor Market in Urban China: Occupational Segregation and Wage Differentials between Urban Residents and Rural Migrants in Shanghai," *Journal of Comparative Economics,* Vol. 29, No. 3, pp. 485–504.

Song, Zheng, Kjetil Storesletten, and Fabrizio Zilibotti, 2011, "Growing Like China," *American Economic Review,* Vol. 101, No. 1, pp. 196–233.

Tyers, R., and F. Lu, 2008, "Competition Policy, Corporate Saving and China's Current Account Surplus," ANU Working Paper in Economics and Commerce (Canberra: Australian National University).

World Bank, 2009, "An Assessment of Poverty and Inequality in China," World Bank Report 47349-CN (Washington: World Bank).

Wu, Xioagang, 2005, "Registration Status, Labor Migration, and Socioeconomic Attainment in China's Segmented Labor Markets," University of Michigan Population Studies Center Research Report 05–579.

CHAPTER 8

Germany: Niche Exports and Improved Competitiveness

VLADIMIR KLYUEV[1]

Germany has had large external surpluses over the past decade, while the public debt level has remained high. Large current account surpluses can be attributed to a confluence of factors, including a cyclical surge in global demand for exports and modest domestic wage growth that has helped strengthen competitiveness. An improvement in the private saving–investment balance has been driven by a decline in investment following the reunification boom and higher precautionary saving. High public debt can be traced in a fundamental sense to reunification efforts and policy measures in response to the financial crisis. Structural policies—including tax and financial sector reforms—could help boost growth and reduce external surpluses. Fiscal space needs to be rebuilt, but the pace of consolidation can be measured.

Germany has a long history of external surpluses, and its fiscal record has been relatively strong except during the period of reunification. Merchandise trade has been in surplus continually since the early 1950s. Meanwhile, the current account has stayed positive, with a few exceptions, notably in the 1990s (Figure 8.1). Germany enjoys a solid reputation for fiscal prudence. Nonetheless, the general government deficit has often exceeded the 3 percent Stability and Growth Pact (SGP) limit, and public debt stands well above the 60 percent ceiling (Figure 8.2). Developments in external and fiscal positions can be viewed across four broad time periods, as described below: pre-unification, reunification, the 2000s, and the financial crisis and its aftermath.

There are considerable similarities between *pre-unification* during the 1980s and the run-up to the recent financial crisis, but also key differences. During both periods, the trade surplus improved dramatically, buoyed by strong global demand. At the same time, national saving increased, helped in part by fiscal consolidation, while private investment declined as a share of GDP. Previous analysis of the reasons for the strong trade performance, coupled with generally subdued growth in output, investment, and employment, pointed to structural rigidities rather than macroeconomic policies (Figure 8.3) (Lipschitz and others, 1989).

---

[1]Vladimir Klyuev is a Senior Economist in the IMF Research Department. This chapter was written with guidance from Emil Stavrev and the support of Eric Bang, David Reichsfeld, and Anne Lalramnghakhleli Moses.

Figure 8.1 Germany: Current Account Balance and Trade Balance *(Percent of GDP)*

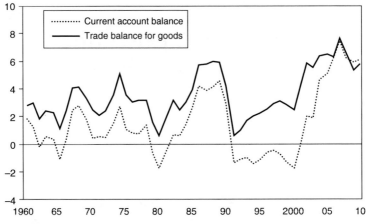

Source: IMF staff calculation.
Note: Pre-1991 data refer to West Germany.

Figure 8.2 Germany: General Government Balance *(Percent of GDP)*

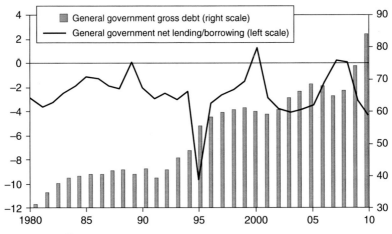

Source: IMF staff estimates.
Note: Pre-1991 data refer to West Germany.

German *reunification* in 1990 had longlasting implications for growth, external balances, and public finances. Efforts to reduce the income gap between east and west (including the one-for-one currency conversion) led to a construction boom and a surge in wages. This was buttressed by generous unemployment support and a narrowing of wage differentials, despite large productivity gaps between the east and the west. At the same time, an increase in fiscal deficits and public debt levels reflected large transfers to the east, a liberal early retirement

Figure 8.3   Germany: Investment Components *(Percent of GDP)*

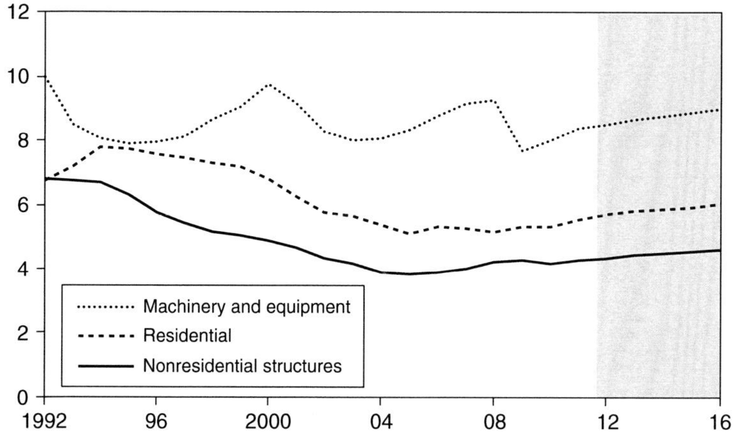

Source: IMF staff estimates.

scheme, and the cost of converting East German enterprises into private firms. Alongside this transition was a shift away from external surpluses to deficits as domestic demand exceeded production.

Subsequent correction of the excesses of the early 1990s laid the groundwork for a stronger external position. Both residential and nonresidential construction declined steadily as a share of GDP. Wage growth slowed, owing to changes in worker bargaining behavior in the face of rising unemployment.[2] And a combination of tax and expenditure measures helped contain fiscal deficits even as the economy decelerated after the unification boom. In the meantime, the consumer price index (CPI)-based real exchange rate depreciated 18 percent in the second half of the 1990s, more than reversing the appreciation that had occurred in the first half of the 1990s.

In *the 2000s,* after a decade of deficits, Germany's external position moved into surplus, while the fiscal position improved in the run-up to the crisis. The current account balance rose sharply from a deficit of 1½ percent of GDP in 2000 to a surplus of 7½ percent in 2007, owing largely, but not exclusively, to an increase in the merchandise trade surplus,[3] noticeably against other euro-area members. The dramatic improvement in the current account primarily reflected a sharp swing in private saving–investment balances.

Net exports contributed about four-fifths of the 9½ percent increase in Germany's real GDP over that period, while domestic demand increased modestly by

---

[2]The unemployment rate climbed steadily from just over 5 percent in 1991 to nearly 10 percent in 1997. See also Decressin and others (2001).

[3]Over that period both exports and imports rose substantially, as German firms extended their production lines into neighboring countries. About 4 percentage points of the increase in the current account was due to a decline in the deficit of the services account and a turnaround in the income account.

around 1½ percent. Despite the export boom and strong corporate profits, private fixed investment declined as a share of GDP by 2½ percentage points. All major investment components declined as a share of GDP between 2000 and 2007, with construction continuing its long post-unification slide (with a tentative recovery starting just before the crisis), while machinery and equipment investment went through a major cycle (Figure 8.3).[4]

Private saving as a share of GDP rose 5¼ percentage points, owing largely to an increase in corporate saving. Household saving increased modestly (one percentage point), even as the labor share of national income fell. In contrast to the large turnaround in the private saving–investment balance, the general government saving–investment balance improved only modestly (by 1¼ percentage points). This was driven by spending cuts (including pension reform and a reduction of unemployment benefits, public-employee fringe benefits, and various subsidies) and supported by strong growth in output and corporate profits. Nonetheless, the ratio of general government debt to GDP has remained in excess of 60 percent since 2002.

The current account and merchandise trade surplus narrowed noticeably during *the financial crisis and its aftermath.* Surpluses are projected to decline further through 2016 in line with maturing global recovery and some deterioration in the terms of trade. The contribution of net exports to real GDP growth is expected to remain positive, but substantially smaller than in the run-up to the crisis.

The crisis delivered a significant blow to public finances. Fiscal deficits reappeared and exceeded 3 percent of GDP in 2009 and 2010, reflecting the impact of automatic stabilizers and a relatively large stimulus. Public debt was also boosted by financial system support measures and peaked at 83½ percent of GDP in 2010. The government has specified a set of consolidation measures, largely on the expenditure side, to bring the fiscal balance in line with its commitments under the SGP, its G20 Toronto commitments, and the national fiscal rule. As a result, the debt ratio is projected to decline to 74½ percent by 2016, which is still above the SGP limit.

ROOT CAUSES OF IMBALANCES

External imbalances in Germany reflect a number of factors, such as improvements in competitiveness, niche exports, low investment rates, and increased national saving. Some of these factors are clearly more important than others. Public debt increased largely due to reunification costs, the weak economy in the first half of the 2000s, and the recent financial crisis.

External Imbalances

The rapid increase in Germany's current account surpluses before the crisis reflects a combination of factors, led by wage behavior and the structure of exports. In

---

[4]It should be noted that in real terms the growth of machinery and equipment investment looks stronger, as its deflator declined relative to the GDP deflator.

particular, favorable product specialization and wage moderation positioned Germany well to take advantage of a cyclical surge in global demand in the years preceding the crisis. Even as exports boomed, the private saving–investment balance improved, as discussed above. Behind this was a slowdown in private investment following the reunification boom and a rise in precautionary saving due to increased policy uncertainty as a result of the reforms in the late 1990s and the early 2000s.

Niche exports allowed Germany to benefit from a cyclical boom in global demand. Exports benefited from strong demand for capital goods, consumer durables, and pharmaceuticals—products in which Germany specializes and enjoys a significant market share (Figure 8.4). Capital goods accounted on average for 45 percent of German merchandise exports in the 2000s, while motor vehicles and parts constituted another 18 percent. Unlike most other advanced economies, Germany was able to maintain its share of key markets, with the rise in world trade translating one-for-one into a rise in German exports.

Wage moderation boosted competitiveness, supporting exports, while dampening domestic demand. Wage growth remained moderate during the expansion, helping firms maintain a competitive edge (Figure 8.5).[5] The euro appreciated nearly 50 percent against the U.S. dollar between 2000 and 2007. However, since

Figure 8.4   Germany: Manufacturing Exports, 1995–2005 *(Percent)*

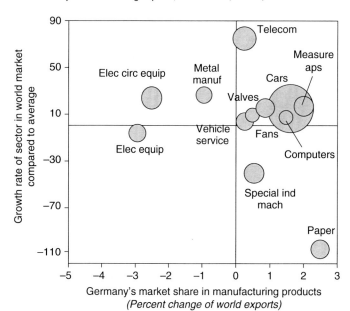

Source: UN Comtrade database.
Note: Size of bubbles is proportional to share in total goods exports. Figure excludes food and chemicals.

---

[5]It should be noted, though, that the importance of competing on price has declined for German exporters.

Figure 8.5 Average Salary per Worker

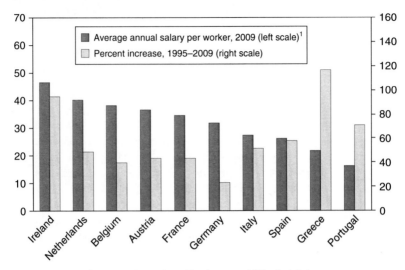

Sources: Organization for Economic Cooperation and Development; and IMF staff calculations.
[1] In thousands of euros.

roughly half of its exports go to other euro-area countries, Germany's nominal effective exchange rate strengthened only 14 percent, the CPI-based real exchange rate only about half of that amount, and the unit-labor-cost-based real effective exchange rate declined slightly by 2007. At the same time, wage moderation resulted in a declining labor income share, which dampened consumption and domestic demand, while boosting net exports by improving relative unit labor costs (Figure 8.6).

Cyclical divergence within the euro area also contributed to intra-area imbalances. Domestic demand in Germany was considerably weaker than demand growth in several euro-area members, notably in the periphery. Thus, the

Figure 8.6 Relative Unit Labor Costs *(Index; 1999 = 100)*

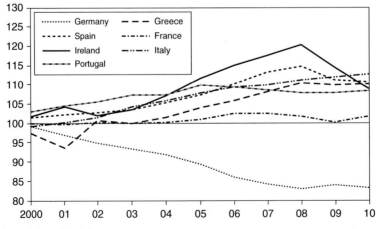

Source: European Commission.

euro-area-wide policy interest rate was arguably too low for the periphery and too high for slow-growing Germany, hindering equilibration of demand across the member states. In addition, because of structural rigidities in the euro area, wage and price adjustments were slow to operate and did not compensate for the lack of an exchange rate adjustment channel.

The private saving–investment balance improved between 2000 and 2007. Both lower investment and higher saving contributed to the large increase in the current account balance before the crisis. Despite booming exports and rising corporate profits, private investment remained particularly lackluster, including relative to Economic and Monetary Union partners. Indeed, investment as a share of GDP declined between 2000 and 2007. This is true not only for construction—which could be attributed to a longlasting hangover from the reunification boom—but also for machinery and equipment. Moreover, as a share of GDP, investment fell not only in services, but also in the booming manufacturing sector. The reasons for low investment in Germany are not entirely clear. Several explanations have been suggested, including uncertainty about the durability of the expansion, gaps and distorted incentives in the financial system, and low productivity growth, particularly in the nontradable sector. Further research would be needed to pin down the reasons behind the low investment rates in Germany, but the three possibilities suggested above can be explained more specifically as follows:.

- *Caution in the face of a surge in external demand.* The weakness of investment possibly reflected the fact that the strong export expansion may not have been viewed as durable. Germany's growth is linked to external developments to a greater extent than in most other large countries, and strong foreign demand may have been viewed as reversible. Indeed, soon after private investment finally started picking up, the global financial crisis broke out.

- *Gaps and distorted incentives in the financial system.* A relatively underdeveloped framework for venture capital and private equity, as well as an inefficient insolvency process, has impeded investment in high-risk, high-growth sectors (Figure 8.7). At the same time, a broader issue concerning access to financing may have played a role, although supporting evidence is limited. In particular, it has been suggested that following the phasing-out of state guarantees, large state-owned banks have been more inclined to invest overseas—including in structured products originated in the United States and in sovereign and bank debt of peripheral euro-area nations, without adequate consideration of risk—rather than financing domestic investment.[6] While there may be some merit to this hypothesis, given high corporate saving and a wide network of savings and cooperative banks that are geared toward financing domestic investment, including small and medium-sized enterprises, the ill-conceived investment strategy of *Landesbanken* may be a more relevant consideration for issues pertaining to financial stability than for access to financing.

---

[6]Arguably, public ownership may have distorted their incentives and account for the lack of a viable business model.

Figure 8.7 Availability of Venture Capital *(Survey index 1–7)*

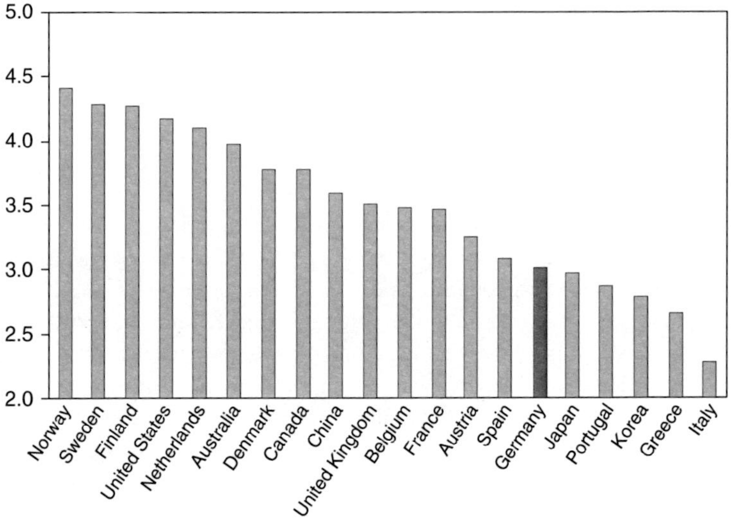

Source: World Economic Forum (2010).

- *Low productivity growth in nontradables.* Germany's labor and total factor productivity growth have been relatively low, dragged down by a lackluster performance of the services sector. Fairly restrictive regulation of professional services (Figure 8.8), remaining barriers to entry and exit of firms, and certain deficiencies in the education system impede productivity growth in the nontradable sector.[7]

Higher saving reflected both public and private sources. National saving rose about 6 percentage points as a share of GDP between 2000 and 2007. Government, corporate, and household saving all increased, as described below.

- *Government saving increased in the years just preceding the crisis.* Fiscal consolidation efforts were undertaken both on the expenditure side (including via pension reform) and on the revenue side (an increase in the value-added tax). In addition, government finances were boosted by rapid growth.

- *High corporate saving reflected an increase in profits during the export boom.* Dividend payouts increased less than profits, possibly because of doubts regarding the sustainability of that boom. High profits did not fuel greater investment but rather were used to strengthen corporate balance sheets. While profitability was helped by wage increases that fell short of productivity

---

[7]The 2010 Organization for Economic Cooperation and Development Economic Survey of Germany identified three main challenges: low tertiary graduation rates among younger cohorts; a vocational training system that provides too much specialized and too little general knowledge, making it hard to adjust to changes in labor demand; and relatively low participation in lifelong learning (OECD, 2010).

Figure 8.8   Regulation in Professional Services

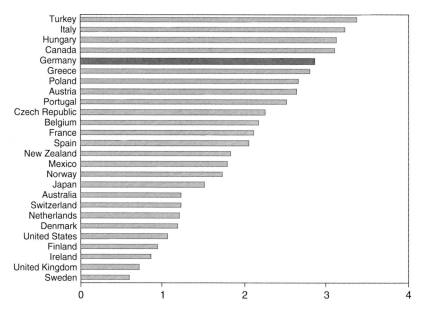

Source: Organization for Economic Cooperation and Development.
Note: The higher the index the stricter the regulation.

growth over a sustained period, there were various factors that encouraged the strengthening of corporate balance sheets. These included changes to the tax regime, changes to the close relationship between corporates and banks, regulatory changes (Basel II), and the increased globalization of production that required access to international bank financing. The effects of regulatory changes and the impact of globalization were likely more pronounced for German corporates due to their heavy reliance on bank-based financing. In contrast to saving, investment was slow to respond. Almost a whole decade of disappointingly low growth, unfavorable demographic trends, and interest rate developments vis-à-vis many European countries likely contributed to the cautious investment response of the corporate sector.

• *The increase in household saving reflects the needs of an aging society and, possibly, policy uncertainty.* Germany has one of the highest household saving rates among member countries of the Organization for Economic Cooperation and Development (OECD), and it remained high even as it declined in many other advanced economies, in some cases spurred by overly easy access to credit. Moreover, after a decade-long post-unification slide, the saving rate rebounded over the course of the 2000s, even as disposable income fell as a share of GDP. This reflects both tradition and the life-cycle needs of an aging society. At the same time, it is quite likely that the rise in household saving also reflects the impact of pension and labor market reforms in the first half of the 2000s, which reduced the generosity of pension and unemployment benefits.

Fiscal Imbalances

The factors leading to accumulation of public debt have shifted over the years. The cost of reunification largely explains the big leap in the debt-to-GDP ratio that occurred in the 1990s. A run-up in debt in the first half of the 2000s was mostly due to the weak economy and attempts to improve growth prospects by cutting taxes. Inter-governmental relations also played a role, with federal cofinancing of regional projects skewing the incentives toward their expansion and resulting in high administrative costs (OECD, 2006).

In addition, the SGP has not prevented Germany from maintaining a debt ratio above 60 percent during the past decade. Between 2008 and 2010, the increase in the debt ratio was largely driven by financial sector support, which added 13 percentage points to the debt-to-GDP ratio. Discretionary measures and cyclical factors also contributed, as the fiscal balance deteriorated by 3.4 percent of GDP due to a combination fiscal stimulus (1.5 percent of GDP in 2009 and 0.7 percent in 2010) and automatic stabilizers, while nominal GDP was nearly unchanged.

ARE GERMANY'S IMBALANCES A PROBLEM?

Factors behind Germany's external surpluses do not primarily reflect market failures or policy-induced distortions. Wage moderation was a reasonable reaction to its earlier excessive growth, which had led to a surge in unemployment, and there is little reason to believe that German institutions or government policies are holding wage growth down. While wage moderation may have led to some overshooting on the competitiveness front, such moderation may well dissipate now that the unemployment rate is at all-time lows. The strong growth of Germany's export markets was a development that was largely exogenous to Germany. Finally, with unfavorable demographic projections, it is not unreasonable for the country to run current account surpluses, although—as IMF staff estimates indicate—they should not be as large as those observed recently (IMF, 2012).

This said, from a domestic perspective there are good reasons for boosting private demand and reducing vulnerability to external shocks. Low output and productivity growth reflect a trend decline in investment relative to GDP (Figure 8.9). The impact is twofold—on demand in the short run and on productive capacity in the longer term.

Specifically, lackluster productivity growth in the nontradable sector dampens growth prospects. An acceleration of productivity in services would strengthen incentives to invest in the sector and also stimulate consumption, boosting domestic demand, by raising permanent income. This would improve the standard of living, while reducing current account surpluses over the medium term.

From an external perspective, Germany has benefited from its dependence on foreign markets, but this makes it more susceptible to external shocks. While exports have so far remained largely isolated from low-wage competition, the country's position is likely to be challenged as emerging market economies move up the technological ladder. Accordingly, this may result in sluggish GDP growth going forward if domestic demand remains weak.

Figure 8.9   Germany: Private-Fixed-Investment-to-GDP Ratio and Potential Growth *(Percent)*

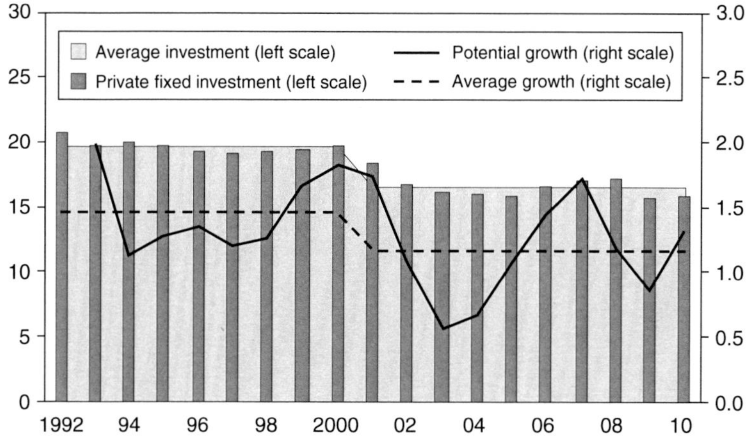

Source: IMF staff calculations.

To some extent, these factors are mutually reinforcing. Weak productivity growth, particularly in the nontradable sector, lowers incentives to invest, holding back potential output and income and thus consumption. In turn, lower domestic demand reduces the incentive to invest, notably in the services sector, thus dampening demand for labor and keeping wages and consumption in check.

High public debt has well-known vulnerabilities associated with it. However, it should be noted that Germany's public debt (both gross and net in percent of GDP) is among the lowest in advanced G20 economies. German bunds continue to be the benchmark asset in the euro area, and credit default swap spreads on German debt remain low. Thus, while fiscal space needs to be reestablished, fiscal consolidation can afford to proceed at a measured pace, helping output recover from the crisis.

Germany's solid fiscal position is essential for maintaining stability in the euro area. Because of its size and history of (relative) fiscal prudence, demonstrated again by the introduction of a Constitution-based structural balance rule, Germany plays a key anchoring role in the euro area. Should investors lose confidence in Germany's creditworthiness, the implications may be severe, with borrowing costs going up all across Europe. In addition, respect for the SGP by the largest member state is important for maintaining stability and budget discipline in the euro area.

HOW TO ADDRESS IMBALANCES

Policy Priorities

A number of factors should reduce Germany's current account surplus going forward. The need for budget consolidation is smaller in Germany than in most of its trading partners, and the smaller fiscal improvement (relative to trading partners) would (all else being equal) lower its current account balance (IMF, 2011, Chapter 4). With anemic growth in advanced economies, the demand for German exports is likely to be low for a protracted period. This may, however, be offset by rising demand from emerging market economies. At the same time, the ongoing increase in productive capacity and technological sophistication of emerging market manufacturers may threaten Germany's competitive position. And with the unemployment rate at its lowest in nearly 20 years and 5 percentage points below its fairly recent peak, wage moderation may be running its course. In fact, wage growth had picked up just prior to the crisis, interrupting a period of wage discipline, but then the crisis put a lid of wages.

Structural policies directed at promoting growth and stability could also help reduce external imbalances and diversify sources of growth. Importantly, policies that increase labor force participation and productivity growth, especially in areas outside Germany's traditional strength, can stimulate consumption and investment. This would shift growth toward domestic demand and reduce Germany's dependence on foreign demand, thus lessening the uncertainty and decreasing vulnerabilities. Ongoing efforts to increase the labor force through greater participation of female and older workers and the migration of skilled workers are welcome. Raising the quality of human capital will require reforms to the system of education and training. Raising productivity in the services sector would be helped by greater competition, including at the regional level in network industries such as transportation and energy. That, in turn, should boost investment, which is key to higher growth and potential output, and lower the need for precautionary saving. Overall, these structural policies, including tax reform, will raise welfare and are likely to lower current account balances over the medium term. Action on several fronts can help achieve these objectives.

Reforming the financial sector will be an essential complement to raise the economy's growth potential and increase its resilience. Broadening the channels of financial intermediation would facilitate the allocation of resources toward innovation and new engines of growth. This would require a greater development of intermediation outside traditional banking channels, using so-called arms-length finance. Changes to regulation and supervision would have to keep pace with the development of a more arms-length system in order to ensure financial stability.

Lower corporate taxation would stimulate investment. While the 2008 corporate income tax reform improved Germany's tax competitiveness, abolishing the inefficient, volatile, and geographically uneven trade tax imposed by municipalities would further reduce the marginal effective tax rate. Further development of venture capital and private equity markets would increase the availability of risk capital, spurring investment and productivity growth. The measures could include (1) removing uncertainties regarding the tax treatment of venture capital firms; (2) redesigning the change-of-ownership rule, which eliminates loss and interest carry-forward; and (3) promoting faster restructuring proceedings for insolvent entities.

Reorienting German banks to serve domestic clients could help increase investment and consumption. While the small institutions (cooperative banks and *Sparkassen*) are domestically oriented, the large, state-owned *Landesbanken* shifted a considerable part of their portfolio abroad in the run-up to the crisis and now find themselves in a difficult situation and in need of government support. Reducing the states' ownership of these institutions (direct and via *Sparkassen*) would spur them to establish a viable business model, which would likely involve greater domestic lending. IMF staff research has found that a smaller public share of the banking system is associated with smaller current account balances (Ivanova, 2012). Even if such reform has an insignificant impact on investment and the current account, it will benefit financial stability.

Less regulation and more measures to improve education would spur productivity growth and domestic demand. In the long run, higher productivity would mean higher output, higher income, and commensurately higher domestic demand without a first-order effect on the current account. However, on the likely protracted transition path, the prospect of higher productivity growth would stimulate additional investment, and higher permanent income would push current consumption up, reducing the trade surplus.

Figure 8.10   Labor Tax Wedge, 2010 *(Percent of labor costs)*

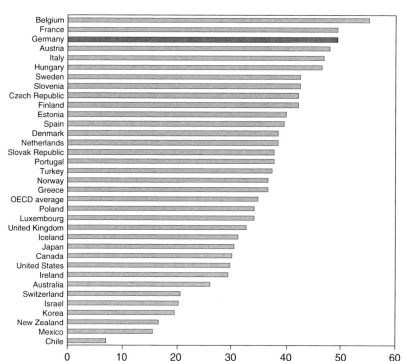

Source: Organization for Economic Cooperation and Development.

The government has identified a set of measures to set the public debt ratio on a declining path. The envisaged pace of consolidation is appropriate, although it could be slowed in case of a substantial negative shock to growth. Fiscal adjustment is anchored by a new limit on structural deficits of the federal and state governments, which is enshrined in the Constitution and should therefore improve national implementation of the SGP.

Within the budget envelope, there is scope for making the adjustment more "growth-friendly." The large labor tax wedge facing low earners could be reduced by introducing in-work and earned-income tax credits or by raising the threshold for low-income tax relief and reducing the speed of benefit withdrawal (Figure 8.10). A reform of the income-splitting regime could improve incentives for labor market participation by secondary earners. Abolishing the inefficient and volatile local trade tax would reduce the burden on corporations, which is among the highest in the world (Figure 8.11). Reduction in direct taxes would promote employment, investment, and growth, and could be paid for by eliminating concessions in the value-added tax, raising property and inheritance taxes, and cutting some poorly targeted social benefits (such as unconditional child support). There is also scope for increasing the efficiency of education spending.

Figure 8.11   Corporate Income Tax Rate, 2011 *(Percent)*

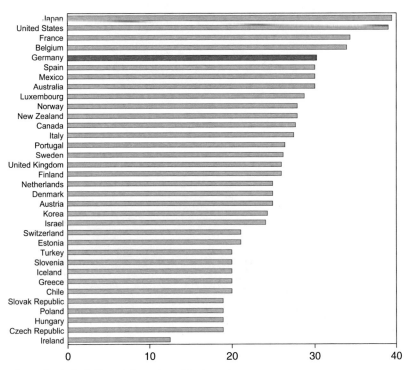

Source: Organization for Economic Cooperation and Development.

TOWARD GLOBAL ACTION

As part of global rebalancing, Germany could contribute to higher and more stable global growth by relying less on exports and more on domestic demand. Increasing the country's domestic demand could raise global growth, while a lower reliance on external sources could contribute to rebalancing and thus to more sustainable global growth.

Structural reform in the services sector could boost productivity and investment, narrowing the large external surplus while enhancing growth potential. In product markets, gradual convergence to best practices in terms of regulations in retail trade and professional services would increase productivity in nontradables and raise investment. In labor markets, improving the availability of child care, along with tax reform, would increase labor participation of secondary-earner, elderly, and low-skilled workers.

Alongside structural reform, tax reform could further support investment and employment, while minimizing distortions. A revenue-neutral tax reform that shifts taxes away from more distortive direct corporate income and personal income taxes to less distortive indirect taxes would help further promote investment, employment, and growth.[8] Tax cuts could be financed by an increase in consumption tax collection achieved by moving toward best practices via eliminating concessions (reduced rates and exemptions) in the value-added tax. These actions to strengthen domestic spending could help support global demand rebalancing and growth.

REFERENCES

Decressin, Jörg, Marcello Estevão, Philip R. Gerson, and Christoph A. Klingen, 2001, "Job-Rich Growth in Europe," in IMF Selected Issues Paper SM/01/307 (Washington: International Monetary Fund).

International Monetary Fund (IMF), 2011, *World Economic Outlook*, September (Washington: International Monetary Fund).

———, 2012, "Staff Report for the 2012 Article IV Consultation," IMF Country Report No. 12/161 (Washington: International Monetary Fund).

Ivanova, Anna, 2012, "Current Account Imbalances: Can Structural Policies Make a Difference?" IMF Working Paper 12/61 (Washington: International Monetary Fund).

Lipschitz, Leslie, Jeroen Kremers, Thomas Mayer, and Donogh McDonald, 1989, *The Federal Republic of Germany: Adjustment in a Surplus Country*, IMF Occasional Paper 64 (Washington: International Monetary Fund).

Organization for Economic Cooperation and Development (OECD), 2006, *Economic Surveys: Germany* (Paris: OECD). www.oecd.org/eco/surveys/36789944.pdf.

———, 2010, *Economic Surveys: Germany* (Paris: OECD). www.oecd.org/germany/economic surveyofgermany2010.htm.

World Economic Forum, 2010, *The Global Information Technology Report, 2009–10* (Geneva: World Economic Forum).

---

[8]For corporations, this includes elimination of municipal trade taxes and introduction of an allowance for the normal return on new equity (to remove the debt bias). For individuals, reforms should target incentives for those marginally attached to the labor force (secondary-earner, elderly, and low-skilled workers), which could have a considerable effect on labor supply. For these groups, incentives should aim to affect the participation margin—the decision of whether to seek employment as opposed to how many hours to work.

CHAPTER 9

Japan: Low Growth and an Aging Population

MITALI DAS[1]

Japan has sustained fiscal deficits over many years that have led to a dramatic increase in public debt. Large fiscal deficits have resulted from persistently low growth—reflecting a trend decline in productivity, a shrinking labor force, and low investment—as well as the needs of a rapidly aging population, and a series of policy missteps. At the same time, private saving has remained high, helping Japan maintain persistent external surpluses. Unsustainable fiscal imbalances pose risks to domestic stability, and also carry risks for the global economy. Growth-enhancing structural reforms (to boost investment and potential growth) and fiscal consolidation measures (through a combination of entitlement reform and tax measures) are needed to reduce imbalances and anchor sustainability.

The collapse of asset markets in the early 1990s marked the origin of a prolonged period of economic stagnation in Japan. From 1973 to 1991, Japan was one of most dynamic economies of the G20, growing at an average annual rate in excess of 4 percent. But growth came to an abrupt halt with the bursting of the asset-market bubble in 1991. Private demand collapsed, leading to repeated fiscal stimulus over a decade to sustain overall demand. Despite steadily widening fiscal deficits and policy rates that were brought down to nearly zero, output remained largely unresponsive, growing at an average annual rate of 1.1 percent from 1991–2001. Japan suffered from a string of negative output gaps and intermittent deflation during the period. Growth improved modestly in 2002–07, averaging 1.8 percent annually, before the financial crisis caused a severe contraction in output.

Low growth, deflation, and large fiscal deficits have had adverse implications for public debt. The steady increase in primary deficits—from an average of 1.7 percent of GDP in the 1990s to an average of 5 percent in 2000–07—is reflected in the evolution of the net debt ratio, which rose from 12 percent of GDP in 1991 to 81 percent in 2007 and from 67 to 188 percent in gross terms.[2] This is by far the highest debt ratio among advanced economies (Figure 9.1).

---

[1]Mitali Das is a Senior Economist in the IMF Research Department. This chapter was written with guidance from Josh Felman and support from Eric Bang, David Reichsfeld, and Anne Lalramnghakhleli Moses.

[2]Net public debt is gross financial liabilities less gross financial assets of the general government (central and local governments, and the social security fund), while gross public debt refers to gross financial

Figure 9.1 Gross Debt for G20 Advanced Countries, 2010 *(Percent of GDP)*

Source: IMF staff calculations.

Figure 9.2 Japan: Structural Balance of the General Government *(Percent of potential GDP)*

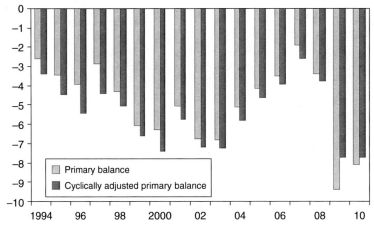

Source: IMF staff calculations.

In the decade following the asset-price collapse, rising deficits were primarily a consequence of increasing expenditures (including fiscal stimulus) and a series of tax cuts, with a lower (relative) contribution from revenues. In the late 1990s, the cyclically adjusted deficit began to widen significantly, as entitlement spending began to rise with an aging population and structurally low revenues played a more significant role (Figure 9.2). The share of social security expenditures in GDP rose from 10 percent in 1991 to 16 percent in 2007.

---

liabilities of the general government. Net public debt is the more relevant concept for long-run debt sustainability, while gross debt is the key indicator from a market perspective, given Japan's large roll-over requirements. The latter measure tends to be more comparable across countries as well.

More recently, the deep recession and the fiscal response that followed the global financial crisis pushed debt to unprecedented levels. Following the crisis, net debt escalated sharply to 130 percent in 2011. The rise in the public debt ratio reflected the combination of a steep decline in nominal output, a drop in revenue, fiscal stimulus (around 2½ percent of GDP in both 2009 and 2010), and automatic stabilizers. Recovery from the financial crisis was interrupted by the March 2011 earthquake, which brought fiscal balances under further pressure. Reconstruction efforts are likely to add fiscal costs of around 3 percent of GDP over the next several years.

Despite substantial public dissaving, Japan's external balance has remained in surplus for over two decades. This has occurred because deteriorating public balances have been roughly offset by rising private sector surpluses (Figure 9.3). In particular, deep structural changes effected by the asset-price collapse led both national saving and national investment to fall about 7 percentage points of GDP between 1992 and 2008. More recently, during the financial crisis, the rapid increase in public expenditure resulted in a much larger decline in national saving than investment, temporarily compressing the external surplus.

The trend decline in national investment has been driven by the private sector. Private capital formation fell from a high of 26 percent of GDP in 1990 to 18 percent in 2008, reflecting deep structural transformations in the economy, including the unwinding of overinvestment in the asset-price-bubble era, a protracted process of corporate deleveraging, and expectations of low growth.

Public investment was a key stimulus measure in the years immediately following the asset-price bust, rising about 2 percentage points of GDP over 1990–95 to 8 percent in 1995. Thereafter, the public investment ratio steadily declined to around 4 percent in 2008, and the share of public investment in stimulus measures was relatively small in the recoveries following the Asian crisis, the dot-com

Figure 9.3   Japan: Sectoral Financial Surplus *(Percent of GDP)*

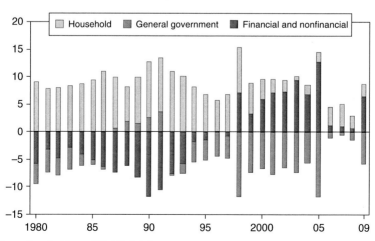

Sources: Haver Analytics; and IMF staff calculations.

bubble crash and the recent financial crisis (where it contributed one-half of a percentage point of GDP in the 2009 stimulus package).

The decline in national saving has been led by large public sector dissaving. In particular, private saving rates ranged between 20 and 26 percent for nearly the entire period of 1990–2008,[3] while gross public saving declined 7 percentage points from 1990–2004, before rising modestly in the years before the financial crisis.

The composition of private saving rates, however, underwent a dramatic reversal during this period. Household saving rates declined from 8 percent of GDP in 1991 to under 3 percent in 2009, reflecting an aging population and stagnating incomes, while corporate saving rates surged from 16 to 21 percent as a result of a sustained drive toward restructuring and favorable financial conditions.

Fiscal imbalances are projected to remain large going forward. Following the global financial crisis and the March 2011 earthquake, IMF staff have projected that a near-term decline in GDP and reconstruction efforts will push the net public debt ratio to 160 percent by 2015 (IMF, 2011a). Reflecting the relatively slow recovery, projections are for private saving imbalances to persist as well at high levels over the medium term.

ROOT CAUSES OF IMBALANCES

The fundamental reasons for major imbalances in Japan's economy and public finances are the long duration of the economic slump and adverse demographics. Large and rising fiscal imbalances in Japan are fundamentally a reflection of persistently low growth. Low growth has spurred public spending and depressed tax revenues over many years, perpetuating a cycle of adverse debt dynamics. Low growth has also made it politically difficult to introduce corrective measures: until recently, Japan had had no major (revenue-raising) tax reforms in more than 20 years. Fiscal imbalances have persisted due to high private saving, strong home bias, and the existence of stable institutional investors.

Anemic Growth

Stagnating output reflects the confluence of a trend decline in total factor productivity (TFP), a shrinking labor force, low capital investment, and inadequate policy adjustment after the asset-price collapse. In real terms, output grew just 25 percent between 1990 and 2007 and the contraction experienced during the recent crisis reduced real output in 2010 to its 2005 level (in nominal terms, to its 1995 level) (Figure 9.4).[4]

---

[3]Private saving abruptly and briefly spiked to 31 percent of GDP in 1998.
[4]As a reference, between 1990 and 2007, real output grew 33 percent in Germany, 37 percent in France, 53 percent in the United Kingdom, 64 percent in the United States, about 300 percent in India, and about 500 percent in China.

Figure 9.4 Japan: Gross Domestic Product *(Trillions of yen; base year 1990)*

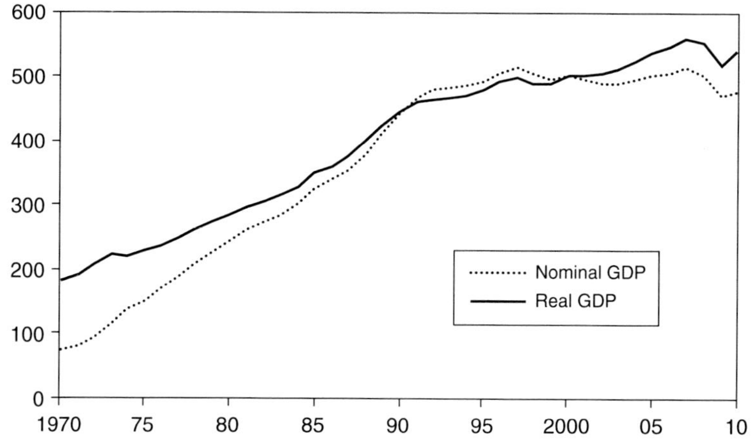

Source: IMF staff calculations.

TFP growth decelerated steadily after the collapse of asset markets in 1991 (Figure 9.5).[5] Japan's low aggregate productivity is largely a consequence of low productivity in services, as manufacturing has witnessed sustained productivity gains over the last decade. The slowdown is significant not just because of its impact on output growth but because, by lowering the expected rate of return on capital, it has hindered private investment. While some of the TFP deceleration may have been inevitable after exhaustion of technological catch-up after the 1980s, policy distortions have played a significant role. These include government policy schemes that subsidize inefficient firms through credit guarantees; barriers to entry in key service industries that inhibit competition and limit incentives for firms to invest in productivity-enhancing technology;[6] and restrictions on inward foreign direct investment (FDI) that limit spillovers such as transfer of technology. Credit guarantees to small and medium-sized enterprises (SMEs) have perpetuated the problem of "zombie" firms that started in the 1990s—namely, inefficient enterprises have lingered, constraining investment by healthier firms.[7]

---

[5]Estimates of TFP over 1990–2008 vary widely, but most economists agree that TFP growth has slowed considerably since the 1990s; see Hayashi and Prescott (2002), Jorgenson and Motohashi (2005), and Naoki (2011). Calculations here are based on a standard Cobb-Douglas production function, with capital share of output set at 0.32 (average from 1980–89).

[6]Services sector investment is notably low in research and development, and particularly in information and communication technology, which was instrumental in accelerating productivity elsewhere (e.g., the United States).

[7]A widespread practice in the 1990s had Japanese banks lending to these unprofitable firms known as "zombies," whose presence discouraged entry and investment by healthier firms. See Caballero, Hoshi, and Kashyap (2008).

Figure 9.5 Japan: Growth Accounting *(Percent)*

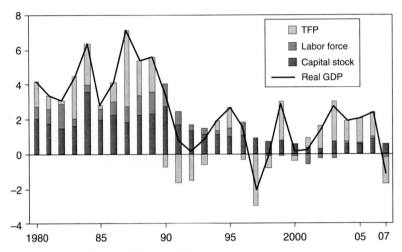

Sources: Japan Cabinet Office; and IMF staff calculations.
Note: TFP = total factor productivity.

Figure 9.6 Japan: Labor Force Size and Participation

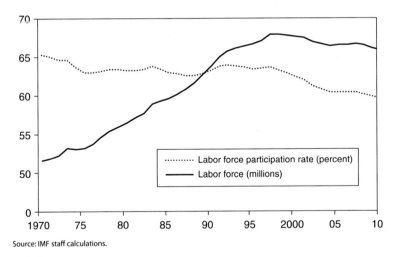

Source: IMF staff calculations.

Demographic change has also been inimical to growth. The growth of Japan's labor force has steadily declined since the early 1990s, turning negative in the early 2000s, with direct consequences for output and growth potential (Figure 9.6). Participation rates have also been on a trend decline. Trends in the labor force reflect an aging population and declining fertility. The share of the elderly in the population rose 14 percentage points from 1980–2010 (in part due to rising longevity), making Japan the oldest as well as the fastest-aging population in the world, while fertility rates fell from 1.75 births per woman to 1.3.[8]

Against this backdrop for productivity and labor, private investment has also been weak. While investment by large manufacturers, particularly in the export sector, has seen brief periods of expansion, investment by SMEs has stagnated for decades. Structural changes in the Japanese economy from lower potential growth to deflation (and its effect on real interest rates) and distortions in the regulatory environment lie behind these trends. Notably, inadequate restructuring of SMEs has held back investment. In the late 1990s, large manufacturing firms restructured aggressively, spurred by pressures from competing in global markets and helped by favorable overseas conditions. However, restructuring in insulated sectors of the domestic economy—notably among SMEs in services—has been much slower. In part, this reflects credit guarantees for SMEs that limit incentives for bank-led workouts and restructuring.[9] As a consequence, balance sheet problems and high leverage have lingered in SMEs, making it difficult for them to secure financing for investment. Meanwhile, the practice of directing the bulk of credit guarantees to established firms has acted as a barrier to entry against new and more productive firms, further restraining investment.

Investment has adjusted to expectations of lower trend growth. The decline in the growth of the labor force, and expectations of a continued slowdown, have implied slower steady-state growth of the capital stock and lower trend growth expectations for the years ahead. Low growth expectations in turn have resulted in a downward adjustment of investment. Export-oriented manufacturing has been less affected by domestic prospects, as its brighter growth prospects, lower production costs, and bigger markets abroad have encouraged firms to substitute FDI for domestic investment.[10] But even in this sector, investment has been subdued barring brief episodes (e.g., 2003–07), while weak domestic prospects have dampened investment demand by domestically oriented firms, notably SMEs in the services sector.

Policy missteps have played a part, too. Monetary policy could have been eased faster in the years following the asset-price collapse. Real policy rates were lowered only gradually, from over 5 percent in 1990 to 1 percent in 1995, providing inadequate stimulus to revive demand and prevent the emergence of deflation. In addition, the stop-start nature of fiscal policy dampened its effectiveness. With only nascent signs of recovery in 1997, fiscal stimulus was withdrawn and a consumption tax to initiate fiscal consolidation was put in place on the eve of the Asian crisis. But the contraction in output that followed the outbreak of the crisis

---

[8]That the decline in the growth rate of output since the asset-price collapse has been much smaller in per capita terms than in level terms only underscores the importance of demographics in Japan.
[9]Credit guarantees to SMEs have ceilings and duration limits from seven to 10 years, but the credit guarantees are sometimes granted with limited evaluation of potential credit risks. See McKinsey Global Institute (2000).
[10]Although outward FDI as a share of GDP is small, the share steadily increased from 0.5 percent of GDP in the 1990s to more than 1 percent over 2000–07.

led to a resumption of stimulus measures. Moreover, weak corporate governance, along with delays in recognizing the severity of nonperforming loans and balance sheet damage for over a decade after the asset-price collapse, also proved costly, both in terms of taxpayer funds and in holding back a recovery, as zombie firms lingered, constraining investment by sound firms.

In the near term, many factors that have contributed to Japan's growth slow-down are likely to persist or intensify. Pressures from demographics are going to increase, concerns about growth expectations will be amplified by the sluggish global recovery and recovery from the earthquake, and major reforms will be needed to comprehensively address much-needed SME restructuring.

Adverse Debt Dynamics

Weak output growth, in turn, has eroded tax revenue collection. A declining revenue share of GDP has played a significant role in the buildup of public debt. This share fell 3 percentage points from the peak of the asset-price bubble to the late 1990s, and then stagnated until the mid-2000s (Figure 9.7). Stagnant revenues in the 1990s resulted from a series of tax cuts, while a narrowing of the household tax base has played an important role since. The household compensation share in GDP was fairly constant from the 1980s through the mid-1990s, but thereafter, with stagnating incomes in the 2000s, it declined 2 percentage points by 2007. As a consequence, the elasticity of household tax revenue vis-à-vis GDP deteriorated (Table 9.1).[11]

Figure 9.7   Japan: Cumulative Contribution to Net Debt *(Percentage points of GDP)*

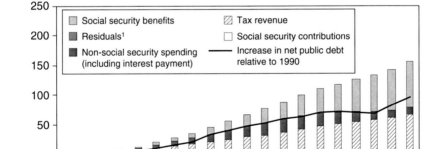

Source: Japan Cabinet Office.
Note: On a general government basis.
[1]Residuals reflect, for example, transfers from outside of the general government.

---

[11]Tax elasticity calculations in this section are done with respect to central government revenue.

TABLE 9.1

Japan: Trends in Tax Elasticity *(Percent average)*						
	1981–85	**1986–90**	**1991–96**	**1997–99**	**2003–07**	**2008–09**
Total tax elasticity	1.29	1.31	−0.96	0.55	4.15	0.97
Household income tax elasticity	1.27	1.56	−5.06	3.48	−2.05	1.77
Corporate tax elasticity	1.34	1.40	−3.87	2.19	8.12	13.59
Household compensation share in GDP	0.54	0.54	0.54	0.53	0.52	0.53
Household property income share in GDP	0.10	0.11	0.11	0.07	0.05	0.05
Corporate profit share in GDP	0.15	0.15	0.17	0.18	0.24	0.23

Sources: Japan Cabinet Office; and IMF staff calculations.
Note: Tax elasticities are vis-à-vis GDP.

Tax buoyancy has also changed. Household tax elasticity in the 1990s was initially large and negative during the period of positive growth, then large and positive during the recession in the late 1990s, as reflected in a significant drop in tax revenues over the decade as a whole. The main reasons appear to be the provision for the deduction of asset market losses and progressivity of the income tax system.[12] From 2003–07, with relatively healthy GDP growth, household tax elasticity vis-à-vis GDP turned large and negative, drawing revenues down further. Decomposing this elasticity into the elasticity of household tax revenues vis-à-vis the household tax base, and the elasticity of the household base itself vis-à-vis GDP, reveals that the deterioration was largely driven by a severe narrowing of the household tax base. In particular, household incomes stagnated even as output grew at a healthy pace, resulting in a significant drop in tax revenues.[13] The high volatility of total tax elasticity over the last two decades is indicative of ongoing structural changes in the economy, and thus gives little indication of the impact of future taxes on future tax revenues.

Further pressure on fiscal balances has come from entitlement spending. Since the early 2000s, Japan's non-social-security spending has been well contained and, at about 16 percent of GDP in 2010 (Figure 9.8), was the lowest among G20 advanced economies. Meanwhile, social security benefits have risen steadily due to population aging. Social security spending rose 60 percent from 1990–2010, accounting for about half of consolidated government expenditure in 2011.[14] Moreover, a sustained increase in the old-age dependency ratio has implied larger social security payments supported by a shrinking pool of workers, which has rapidly deteriorated the social security balance.[15]

[12]See Mühleisen (2000), who notes that loss carry-forwards may have depressed corporate tax elasticity in the mid-1990s.
[13]While the corporate tax base has progressively grown since the 1990s, it is significantly smaller than the household tax base.
[14]Estimates put old-age-related expenditures at about 70 percent of social security spending.
[15]The social security system is partially funded. The social security balance refers to the difference between social security contributions (plus government transfers) and social security payments.

Figure 9.8 Japan: Distribution of General Government Expenditures *(Trillions of yen)*

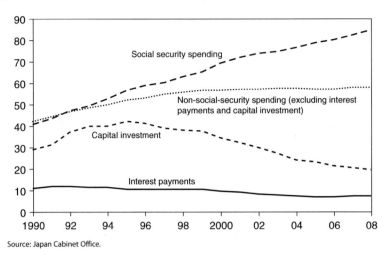

Source: Japan Cabinet Office.

Private Saving Imbalances

The high aggregate private saving rate embeds a deep imbalance. In particular, it reflects a high corporate saving rate, which trended up from 13 percent of GDP in 1981 to 21 percent in 2009, and a very low household saving rate, which declined from 10 percent of GDP to less than 3 percent over the same period (Figure 9.9).[16] Spending retracted during the financial crisis, pushing the private saving rate up to 23 percent in 2009, highest among the advanced G20 countries.

The decline in household saving rates reflects a rapidly aging population and the stagnation of household incomes. After growing at an average annual rate of 5 percent in the 1980s, nominal disposable income growth slowed to an average 2 percent in the 1990s and was flat from 2002–07. Stagnating household disposable income has been accompanied by a rising consumption share of disposable income and declining saving among younger households, which has reinforced dissaving by elderly households.

The rise in corporate saving reflects a sustained drive toward restructuring after the excessive indebtedness built up during the asset-price bubble, and has been facilitated by wage moderation and a long period of low interest rates. Strong demand from China, and periods of real effective depreciation associated with deflation and a weak yen, along with the strong and stable income balance from corporate overseas operations, contributed to a sharp rise in profitability (measured by asset turnover and profit margins) for a sustained period between 2002 and the start of the financial crisis.[17] The increase in corporate gross saving led to

---

[16]The evidence indicates that households partially pierced the corporate veil in this period. See Box 9.1.

[17]See Kang, Tokuoka, and Syed (2009) for a more detailed discussion of this period of corporate profitability.

Figure 9.9 Japan: Private Sector Saving Rates *(Percent of GDP)*

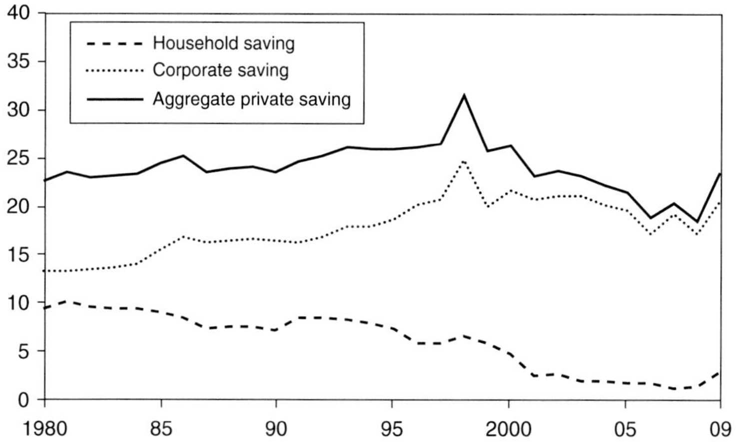

Sources: Japan Cabinet Office; and IMF staff calculations.

BOX 9.1

Have Japanese Households "Pierced the Corporate Veil"?

The striking decline in household saving rates over the period from 1981 to 2009—and by approximately the same magnitude as the increase in the corporate saving rate—suggests that Japanese households "pierced the corporate veil" by adjusting their own saving plans to offset the saving by corporates on their behalf. The argument is that, as ultimate owners of firms, sophisticated shareholders understand that an increase in corporate saving (retention of earnings rather than paying them out as dividends) increases their own net worth and reduces their private saving, re-optimizing in accordance with the life-cycle model of consumption.

Well-known limits to this theory are that households may be myopic, liquidity-constrained, and imperfectly informed about changes in corporate saving, as well as have differential propensities to consume out of wealth versus disposable income. Furthermore, even if shareholder households successfully pierce the corporate veil, their marginal propensities to save may be different from nonshareholder households (Poterba, 1987). In Japan's case, specifically, the corporate veil argument may be harder to rationalize because the share of equities and trusts held by households is about 10 percent of total household wealth (compared to 40 percent in the United States and 20 percent in other G5 economies).

Nevertheless, determining whether household and corporate saving in Japan is indeed fungible is ultimately an empirical question. Ongoing regression analysis indicates that Japanese households' piercing of the corporate veil is incomplete. In particular, a ¥1 increase in corporate saving reduces household saving by between ¥0.65 and ¥0.8.[1] These estimates are higher than the estimated degree of substitutability between U.S. households and corporates (Poterba, 1987).

---

[1]Regression of household saving rates (as a percent of disposable income) on covariates that include corporate saving (share of GDP), household wealth (share of GDP), output gap, old-age dependency ratio, dividend payout (share of GDP), and the real interest rate.

Figure 9.10 Japan: Nonfinancial Gross Saving and Payments *(Percent of GDP)*

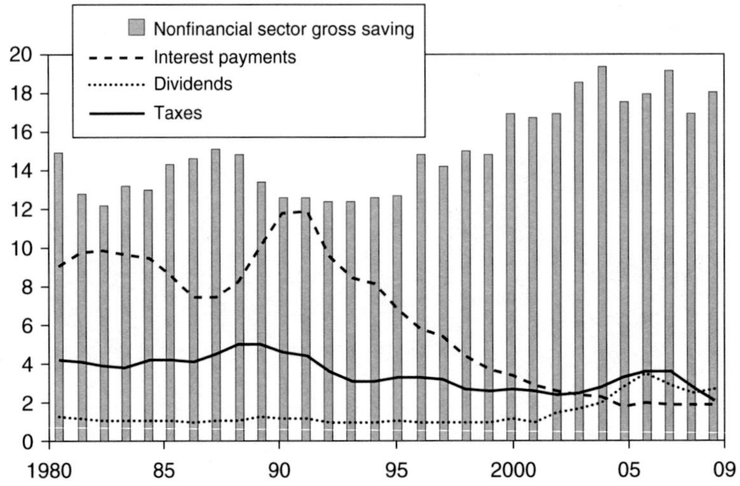

Sources: Japan Cabinet Office; and IMF staff calculations.

a rise in corporate excess saving (i.e., net lending) as well, reversing many years of net borrowing through the 1980s and 1990s.

Globalization of labor and product markets and deregulation in domestic markets have restrained wage growth. Real wages stagnated, growing just 1 percent from 1996–2007. As a consequence, the labor income share dropped from 65 percent in 1991 to 60 percent in 2005 (Sommer, 2009). These wage developments must be viewed in the context of a longer-term decline in the labor income share in advanced economies. In particular, historically, Japan's labor income share was significantly higher than that in other advanced economies. But it has since declined and is now at the G7 average. The integration of large emerging market economies into the global economy facilitated the relocation of manufacturing to regions with low production costs, keeping manufacturing wages flat despite impressive gains in productivity. In nontradables, stagnating productivity and a rapid rise in the hiring of temporary, low-wage, and nonregular workers (facilitated by deregulation) put downward pressure on wages in Japan, which helped maintain lower wages in the tradable sector as well.

Favorable financial conditions also aided the rise in nonfinancial corporate saving (Figure 9.10).[18] The surge in profits was partly a result of a striking decline in interest payments, which dropped from 12 percent of GDP in 1991 to less than 2 percent in 2009, reflecting both lower borrowing rates and a protracted process of corporate deleveraging. Corporate profitability and saving were also boosted by lower tax payments, resulting from a decline in statutory corporate tax

---

[18]The gross saving ratio in the financial sector was on a mild upward trend between the asset-price bust and 2009, and did not contribute significantly to the large increase in corporate saving.

rates since the late 1980s and stagnant dividend payouts, which have persisted between 1–2 percent of GDP in periods of stress as well as in boom years. Corporates have also devoted an increasingly smaller share of profits to upgrading or expanding their capital stock. Japanese nonfinancial corporates were net borrowers continuously from 1980–97, but then increased their net lending position from 1 percent of GDP in 1998 to 5 percent in 2009. Notably, in this time period, slightly more than half the increase in net lending emerged from a decline in capital investment rather than an increase in saving.

Against a backdrop of high profitability, the subdued level of nonfinancial corporate investment is tied to both cyclical and structural factors. From a cyclical standpoint, corporates may have viewed high profitability as unlikely to be sustained going forward and, thus, held back investment in light of growth expectations. This appears to be corroborated in the Bank of Japan's Tankan surveys conducted during 2003–07, where firms revealed relatively subdued growth in sales.

More structurally, corporates may have increased saving to reduce dependence on external financing. Faced with high debt ratios since the collapse of asset markets, Japanese nonfinancial corporates have used profits to repay debt. Moreover, concerns about vulnerability to volatile financial market conditions have spurred firms to reduce their dependence on external financing. This is supported by Tankan surveys that reveal that, since 2003, only a small majority of corporates have viewed lending conditions as accommodative.

Private Saving Financing Public Dissaving

Despite the large and increasing public debt, the government's interest burden has remained low. Between 1992 and 2009, the net debt ratio rose about a 100 percentage points while nominal yields on 10-year Japanese government bonds (JGBs) steadily declined and stabilized at less than 2 percent (Figure 9.11).[19] These developments in the government bond market reflect the confluence of several factors. In effect, while high private saving (equivalently, low private spending) has forced a government that wants to maintain output to run large deficits, low risk appetite and the strong home bias of institutional investors[20] has led to a large domestic base for JGBs that has enabled the government to finance its debt at very low cost.[21] Notably, in 2009, 95 percent of outstanding JGBs were held by domestic financial institutions and households. Without recourse to this

---

[19]Given mild deflation (consumer price index inflation averaged −0.3 percent from 2000–10), real long-term bond yields have also been low, ranging from 0.1 to 2.7 percent over the same period (calculated as nominal long-term bond yields less CPI inflation).

[20]This includes banks, pension funds, and life insurance funds, where the vast majority of household financial assets are held.

[21]Some argue that historically high real estate prices in Japan have encouraged private investors, notably households, to accumulate JGBs to achieve the correct portfolio balance between risky assets (i.e., housing) and safe assets (Iwaisako, Mitchell, and Piggot, 2004). The share of currency and deposits in households' financial assets was 55 percent in 2008.

Figure 9.11 Holdings of Japanese Government Bonds, as of end-2009

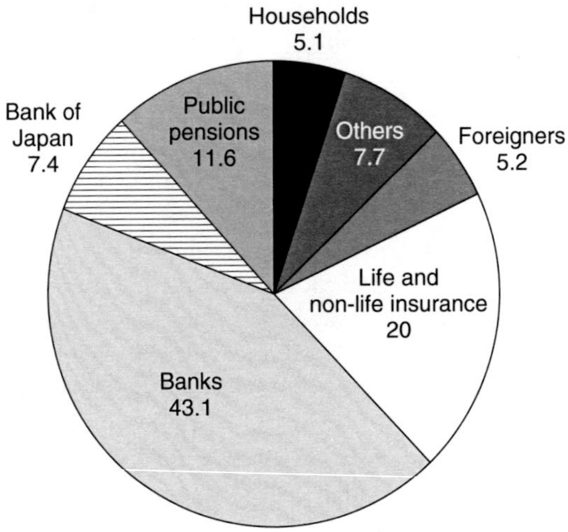

vast pool of savings, funding costs and debt service would have arguably risen faster, and possibly forced an earlier resolution of fiscal imbalances.

Government-owned saving and insurance institutions have provided a captive domestic base for government financing needs. Japan Post Bank and Japan Post Insurance remain fully government-owned and, until 2007, were not subject to regulation by the Financial Services Authority under the same set of rules, risk controls, and disclosure as other financial institutions. In return, funds have been required to be invested in safe assets, particularly JGBs.[22] The recent suspension of plans to privatize Japan Post and proposals to double its deposit ceiling potentially increases the demand for JGBs. At the same time, it threatens to increases the size of an already large financial institution, raising the potential for systemic risk.

In summary, large fiscal and private saving imbalances primarily reflect Japan's inability to resolve multiple structural weaknesses. Low and declining trend growth, low productivity, mild deflation, and the declining labor force must be tackled simultaneously, given that these structural weaknesses are mutually reinforcing.

ARE JAPAN'S IMBALANCES A PROBLEM?

Large fiscal imbalances pose risks to domestic stability and also carry risks for global external positions and sovereign bond markets.

---

[22]As of end-2010, Japan Post Bank held about 76 percent of its assets in JGBs (amounting to 19 percent of outstanding JGBs), and Japan Post Insurance held about 66 percent of its assets in JGBs (amounting to about 8 percent of outstanding JGBs).

Domestic Risks

Should JGB yields rise from current levels, Japanese debt could quickly become unsustainable. Recent events in other advanced economies have underscored how quickly market sentiment toward sovereigns with unsustainable fiscal imbalances can shift. In Japan, two scenarios are possible. In one, private demand would pick up, which would lead the Bank of Japan to increase policy rates, in which case the interest rate–growth differential might not change much. The other is more worrisome. Market concerns about fiscal sustainability could result in a sudden spike in the risk premium on JGBs, without a contemporaneous increase in private demand. An increase in yields could be triggered by delayed fiscal reforms, a decline in private saving (e.g., if corporate profits decline), a protracted slump in growth (e.g., related to the March 2011 earthquake), or unexpected shifts in the portfolio preferences of Japanese investors. Once confidence in sustainability erodes, authorities could face an adverse feedback loop between rising yields, falling market confidence, a more vulnerable financial system, diminishing fiscal policy space, and a contracting real economy.

With regard to public balance sheets, with exceptionally low nominal yields on JGBs, interest payments in 2010 were still 2 percent of GDP (Figure 9.12). An increase of just 100 basis points in average yields would raise the interest bill by an additional 2 percent of GDP, or more if there were a contemporaneous increase in debt. Absent an offsetting effect from more rapid growth, debt dynamics could deteriorate precariously.

As regards private balance sheets, a JGB bond shock, particularly if accompanied by an equity price drop, would imply large capital losses for the principal creditors, which are Japanese banks and pension funds. Capital losses could raise

Figure 9.12   Japan: Public Debt and Interest Payments *(Percent of GDP)*

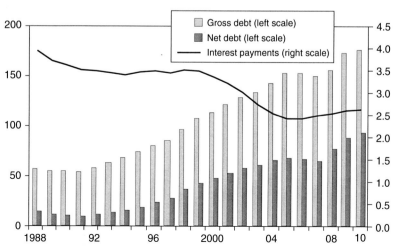

Source: IMF staff calculations.

counterparty risks and force banks into abrupt deleveraging. IMF staff analysis suggests that if the shock is sufficiently large, bank credit would contract as well (IMF, 2011b). Moreover, should banks' deleveraging extend to their positions abroad, exchange rate appreciation could follow, further squeezing aggregate demand.[23]

Multilateral Perspective

A spike in JGB yields could result in an abrupt withdrawal of liquidity from global capital markets and possibly disruptive adjustments in exchange rates. Japan's private net international investment position is significant at about $1.5 trillion, consisting primarily of the outward investments of banks, life insurers, and corporate pension funds. Capital losses following a spike in JGB yields could trigger rapid deleveraging from positions abroad.

In the event of a rise in JGB yields, Japanese banks may need to cut their foreign credit lines. For example, analysis in the IMF 2011 Spillover Report for Japan indicates that an extreme shock (e.g., a 450 basis-point increase) would cut Japan's credit to foreign borrowers by close to 50 percent, assuming that foreign loans are cut first. G20 economies, notably the United Kingdom and Korea, would be among the most exposed to the loss in funding (IMF, 2011b).[24] Also, given evidence from past bouts of global turmoil, abrupt adjustments in exchange rates of major economies are likely to follow.

Finally, the rise in JGB yields could put upward pressure on sovereign yields elsewhere. The risk of transmission of sovereign debt shocks has increased considerably since the 2008 crisis, including from Japan to other sovereigns. Contagion could thus translate a rise in JGB yields into higher interest rates elsewhere. Sovereign bond yields in economies where public debt is already high tend to be the most vulnerable.

HOW TO ADDRESS IMBALANCES

To address imbalances and anchor strong, sustainable, and balanced growth, Japan needs to undertake growth-enhancing structural reforms and growth-friendly fiscal consolidation. Over time, these reforms should help close the output gap, thereby helping to end deflation, encourage investment, and rebalance the economy toward domestic demand. In the short run, however, a key challenge will be to fiscally consolidate while minimizing the negative effects on aggregate demand.

---

[23]If the risk premium shock were accompanied by an equity price drop, large capital outflows by residents could induce net depreciation and offset some of the decline in demand.

[24]As emphasized in IMF (2011b), however, it must be noted that since Japan's cross-border banking links are relatively limited, a sudden withdrawal of funding from Japan, in isolation, is unlikely to threaten systemic stability of any other banking system.

Growth-Enhancing Structural Reforms

Raising productivity is crucial to raising Japan's potential growth over the medium term. Policy priorities include restructuring SMEs and reducing barriers to entry (particularly for start-ups) to improve productivity in services; removing distortions that impede investment; and raising labor force participation. Anticipation of higher productivity could itself encourage business investment, strengthening aggregate demand. These three priorities are developed in more detail below.

- *Strengthening competition in the services sector.* To strengthen competition and raise productivity in insulated industries, Japan needs regulatory reforms that lift barriers to entry in key service industries (medical care, education, transport, utilities); policies that encourage competition, including through stronger penalties for antitrust violations; broader trade and financial liberalization (such as participation in the Trans Pacific Partnership); and weaker restrictions on inward FDI (e.g., lower equity restrictions and easing merger and acquisition rules) (OECD, 2006).

- *Restructuring SMEs and phasing out credit guarantees.* Establishing asset management companies to purchase distressed loans would promote bank-led restructuring and reduce SME leverage. Phasing out credit guarantees and assisting the exit of unproductive SMEs would remove a key barrier to entry for more efficient firms and create space for new investment.

- *Raising labor force participation.* Japan has the lowest level of female labor force participation among member countries of the Organization for Economic Cooperation and Development (OECD), reflecting in part the lack of childcare services and unfavorable tax treatment that discourages female labor participation. Reducing dualism in the labor market, increasing childcare services, and reforming aspects of the tax code that reduce work incentives for secondary earners would encourage more women to join the workforce. The labor force could also be increased by allowing for greater immigration.

Fiscal Consolidation

The Fiscal Management Strategy adopted by the government in June 2010 is a step in the right direction, but a more ambitious strategy is required to maintain confidence in public finances. The government's plans—including targets for halving the primary deficit (in percent of GDP) by 2015, raising the consumption tax rate from 5 to 10 percent, increasing the pension retirement age, and adjusting pension benefits for deflation—are welcome. Further tax reform has also been announced more recently in 2013. However, the plans do not specify steps beyond 2015 for meeting the final of reducing the debt ratio starting in 2021 at the latest.

Given limited scope for cutting expenditures, fiscal adjustment would need to rely mainly on new revenue sources and limits on spending growth. Japan's non-social-security spending is lowest among G20 advanced economies and capital spending has fallen to modest levels, leaving little room for spending cuts. Meanwhile, tax revenue is among the lowest in the advanced G20 economies, primarily reflecting lower consumption and personal income tax revenue.

Among various revenue measures, raising the consumption tax (the value-added tax –VAT) is the most appealing. The consumption tax rate in Japan, at 5 percent, is the lowest among the advanced G20 countries. IMF staff analysis indicates that a gradual increase in the consumption tax from 5 to 15 percent over several years could provide roughly half of the fiscal adjustment needed to put the public debt ratio on a downward path within the next several years.[25] Raising the VAT would dampen growth in the short run, but this could be offset over time by improved confidence in the fiscal outlook.[26] Containing public spending growth and reforming pension entitlements in line with rising life expectancy could generate additional saving. IMF staff analysis indicates that freezing central government contributions to the public pension system in nominal terms, including by raising the pension retirement age (currently 65), could yield 1/2 percent of GDP in savings over 10 years (IMF, 2011b). Additional saving would come from freezing non-social-security spending in nominal terms and introducing caps on social transfers.

TOWARD GLOBAL ACTION

To best contribute to healthier global growth and rebalancing, Japan needs both fiscal adjustment and structural reform. Fiscal adjustment would depress growth in the short run, while structural reforms could buoy growth after a transitional period during which the measures take hold and begin to produce positive effects. While consolidation would likely strengthen the current account surplus, it would significantly reduce attendant risks tied to fiscal sustainability concerns down the road. Growth effects could be particularly severe if Japan were hit by a sovereign risk premium shock. Possible policy elements toward contributing to an upside scenario would include both fiscal consolidation and structural reform.[27]

A comprehensive and simultaneous approach toward fiscal consolidation and structural reforms could be mutually reinforcing and generate considerable gains in growth over the medium term. Although fiscal consolidation has short-term costs, the potential long-term benefits are considerable and reforms that raise potential growth could support consolidation.

---

[25]See Keen and others (2011) for more information on the recommended adjustment strategy.
[26]Relative to the no-adjustment case, IMF staff estimates are that a gradual increase of the VAT (alongside other fiscal consolidation measures) would reduce growth modestly (compared to the baseline) by 0.3–0.5 percentage points per year in the near term but carry long-term benefits. See IMF (2011b)
[27]Preliminary simulations by the OECD (2006) show that if reforms were implemented rapidly, they could add about 0.7 percentage points to growth within a few years. This assumes that Japan's framework gradually converges to best practices in terms of barriers to FDI, regulation of network industries, and barriers to entry in services (especially retail trade and professional services). Further work could explore the implications of restructuring SMEs.

REFERENCES

Caballero, R., T. Hoshi, and A. Kashyap, 2008, "Zombie Lending and Depressed Restructuring in Japan," *American Economic Review*, Vol. 98, No. 5, pp. 1943–977.

Hayashi, F., and E. Prescott, 2002, "The 1990s in Japan: A Lost Decade," *Review of Economic Dynamics,* Vol. 5, No. 1, pp. 206–35.

International Monetary Fund (IMF), 2011a, "Japan—Staff Report for the 2011 Article IV Consultation," IMF Country Report 11/181 (Washington: International Monetary Fund).

———, 2011b, "Spillover Report for the 2011 Article IV Consultation (Japan)," SM/11/143 (Washington: International Monetary Fund).

Iwaisako, T., O. Mitchell, and J. Piggot, 2004, "Strategic Asset Allocation in Japan: An Empirical Evaluation," Wharton School Pension Research Council Working Paper 2005-1 (Philadelphia: University of Pennsylvania).

Jorgenson, D.W., and K. Motohashi, 2005, "Information Technology and the Japanese Economy," *Journal of the Japanese and International Economies*, Vol. 19, No. 4, pp. 460–81.

Kang, K., K. Tokuoka, and M. Syed, 2009, "'Lost Decade' in Translation: What Japan's Crisis Could Portend about Recovery from the Great Recession," IMF Working Paper 09/282 (Washington: International Monetary Fund).

Keen, Michael, Mahmood Pradhan, Kenneth Kang, and Ruud de Mooij, 2011,"Raising the Consumption Tax in Japan: Why, When, How?" IMF Staff Discussion Note 11/13 (Washington: International Monetary Fund).

Mckinsey Global Institute, 2000, *Why the Japanese Economy is Not Growing: Micro Barriers to Productivity Growth* (Washington: Mckinsey Global Institute).

Mühleisen, M., 2000, "Too Much of a Good Thing? The Effectiveness of Fiscal Stimulus," in *Post-Bubble Blues,* ed. by T. Bayoumi and C. Collyns (Washington: International Monetary Fund).

Naoki, Shinada, 2011, "Quality of Labor, Capital and Productivity Growth in Japan: Effects of Employee Age, Seniority and Capital Vintage," RIETI Discussion Paper 11-E-036 (Tokyo: Research Institute of Economy, Trade and Industry).

Organization for Economic Cooperation and Development (OECD), 2006, *Supporting Japan's Policy Objectives: OECD's Contribution* (Paris: OECD).

Poterba, J.M., 1987, "Tax Policy and Corporate Saving," *Brookings Papers on Economic Activity* 2, pp. 455–515 (Washington: The Brookings Institution).

Sommer, M., 2009, "Why are Japanese Wages So Sluggish?" IMF Working Paper 09/97 (Washington: International Monetary Fund).

PART IV

Rebalancing
and Growth

CHAPTER 10

A Roadmap for Collective Action

KRISHNA SRINIVASAN, HAMID FARUQEE, AND EMIL STAVREV[1]

The sources of external imbalances in the run-up to the financial crisis vary widely across the seven systemic economies studied here, largely reflecting factors that have led domestic saving behavior to differ significantly. The case studies indicate that global imbalances have been driven primarily by saving imbalances—generally too low in advanced deficit economies and too high in emerging surplus economies—owing to a combination of equilibrium factors (demographic patterns), structural weaknesses, and domestic distortions. This implies that corrective steps at the national level as discussed in each country chapter—as part of collaborative action to address structural impediments and underlying distortions—will be needed to better support G20 growth objectives.

UNDERSTANDING IMBALANCES

In a nutshell, as shown in Figure 10.1, current account deficits before the crisis reflected low public and private saving (United Kingdom and United States) or low public saving, which was partly offset by high private saving (France and India). Surpluses, on the other hand, reflected high national saving, owing in particular to exceptionally high private saving that exceeded high private investment (China) or to positive private saving–investment balances owing to high saving and low investment that has offset high or modest public dissaving (Japan and Germany).

Abstracting from the financial crisis—which adversely affected budget balances in all countries—a variety of structural and equilibrium factors reflecting country circumstances have driven public saving behavior. These will need to be addressed to reduce external imbalances and bolster public finances. In particular, factors underpinning fiscal deficits include:

- Persistently low growth (making it difficult to balance the budget), reflecting a decline in productivity, a shrinking labor force, and low investment, as well as the needs of a rapidly aging population (Japan);

[1]Krishna Srinivasan is an Assistant Director in the IMF European Department; Hamid Faruqee is a Division Chief and Emil Stavrev is a Deputy Chief in the IMF Research Department. This chapter was written with input from Derek Anderson, Michal Andrle, Mika Kortelainen, Dirk Muir, Susanna Mursula, and Stephen Snudden, and with the support of Eric Bang, David Reichsfeld, and Anne Lalramnghakhleli Moses.

Figure 10.1   Elements of Imbalances

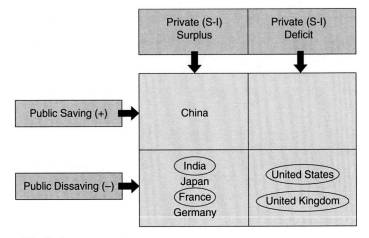

Source: IMF staff estimates.
Note: Countries circled denote those with current account deficits.

- Structural imbalances between tax revenues and spending commitments prior to the crisis, underfunded entitlement obligations, the lack of agreement on fiscal adjustment priorities, and the lack of fiscal rules and strict enforcement mechanisms to impose sufficient budgetary discipline (France, United Kingdom, and United States).

- Political economy considerations exerting strong pressure on spending and resistance to raising taxes (India, Japan, and United States), a weak revenue system, and financial repression (India).

At the same time, domestic policy distortions (defined broadly as factors that impede a market from equilibrating) have also played an important role in driving imbalances. Distortions, for example, have helped fuel public dissaving in some emerging deficit economies. In India, tight financial restrictions have allowed the perpetuation of large fiscal deficits.

Distortions in financial systems have fueled low private saving and large current account deficits. Weak private saving–investment imbalances before the crisis, reflecting underlying problems in financial sectors, have played a role in fueling current account deficits in major advanced economies, notably the United States and United Kingdom. In particular, distortions in the financial system pertaining to regulatory and supervisory frameworks were partly responsible for a fundamental breakdown in market discipline and mispricing of risk (reflected in credit and housing booms) and contributed to a widening of external imbalances. In the United Kingdom, constraints on the supply of housing precluded a construction boom but further fueled a house price boom, which, in turn, contributed to low household saving and high private debt.

High national saving in China reflects significant underlying distortions. Policy distortions or gaps—reflecting inadequate social safety nets, restrictive financial conditions, an undervalued exchange rate, subsidized factor costs, limited dividends, and lack of competition in product markets—have underpinned exceptionally high national saving and, in turn, current account surpluses in China. Large current account and balance of payment surpluses have led to massive reserve accumulation in China (and elsewhere),[2] contributing to the low-cost financing of U.S. current account deficits.

Weak investment in some advanced economies also reflects policy distortions. Modest external surpluses in Japan are a result in part of favorable private saving–investment balances (e.g., demographics), but distortions have also contributed, as private investment growth (particularly by small and medium-sized enterprises) has remained weak, while corporate saving has remained large. Similarly, for Germany, large external surpluses reflect, in part, favorable private saving–investment balances, but distortions in the financial sector may be a drag on domestic investment.

POLICY IMPLICATIONS

Broadly speaking, saving imbalances—too low in major advanced economies and too high in key emerging surplus economies—imply that policymakers need to proceed with a greater sense of urgency to facilitate dual rebalancing acts: a hand-off from public-demand-led to private-demand-led growth in major advanced economies; and a shift from growth led by domestic demand toward external demand in major advanced deficit economies, and vice versa in major emerging surplus economies. Overall, external rebalancing has been modest, partly due to the global recession and insufficient policy effort. To facilitate better adjustment, efforts will be needed to tackle the underlying distortions that are the reason for high saving in some surplus members.

Actions on several fronts would facilitate greater rebalancing of global demand to support growth and enhance welfare. Specifically, as detailed in the case studies, policies tailored to individual country circumstances and aimed at addressing underlying distortions are needed to facilitate the dual rebalancing acts and to anchor countries' growth objectives. On a broad level, two key actions, among others, are needed:

- Appropriately timed and paced fiscal consolidation across major advanced economies, including France, Japan, the United Kingdom, and the United States, as well as in India, to reduce persistent deficits, create policy space, and anchor sustainability. This is currently in progress in many of these economies. Fiscal consolidation will, however, depress growth in the near term. Hence, closing the output gap will require complementary policies through greater G20 collaboration (see below).

---

[2]One channel through which China's reserve accumulation policy could affect reserve accumulation policies in other emerging market economies is through exchange rates, as they are competing in similar product markets.

- To offset weaker demand in major advanced partner countries, increased internal demand elsewhere, notably China (and other surplus countries) to support domestic and global growth. This will require lower national saving in China, notably by reducing the distortions that have kept saving exceptionally high. To avoid overheating, China's net exports will have to moderate, implying a lower current account surplus. There is also room to bolster domestic demand by reducing private saving–investment balances in Japan and Germany, particularly by lowering corporate saving and boosting investment by reducing distortions.

COLLECTIVE ACTION

Against a backdrop of weaker global growth and heightened downside risks, there is an urgent need for stronger and more complementary policy action by the G20 membership to secure economic expansion. As highlighted by the country case studies, assessments of imbalances indicate the need for domestic policies and strengthened collaborative action to anchor growth over the medium term and to avoid damaging setbacks to the recovery. Thus, an "upside scenario" is developed that brings together these elements. While G20 baseline policies have strengthened over the past few years, further collective action on three key policy fronts—fiscal, structural, and other rebalancing policies—would be desirable. This collective effort would reduce problem imbalances and support growth, mitigating key risks while avoiding a "demand deficit" that could derail the global expansion.

Contours of Global Action

Strengthened collective policy action on key fronts will be needed to achieve the G20's shared growth objectives and to reduce major imbalances. The overall assessment based on the country studies in this volume suggests three key policy areas for further action.

First, greater medium-term fiscal consolidation is needed in major advanced deficit countries to restore the sustainability of public finances. The review of policy commitments suggests that greater consolidation is necessary in the context of credible and realistic medium-term fiscal frameworks in order to anchor shared growth objectives. This assessment is supported by IMF staff's analysis of G20 macroeconomic frameworks, which suggests that the anticipated improvement of public finances is partly predicated on optimistic growth projections by the authorities that may not fully materialize, according to IMF staff baseline growth projections. Finally, the country studies also suggest that additional fiscal adjustment will be needed to help reduce persistently moderate or large external imbalances in key deficit economies through higher national saving.

Second, further structural reform is needed to support growth, particularly in advanced surplus economies. In addition to near-term efforts to reduce high unemployment and financial sector repair and reform to support the private sector recovery, further action is needed to enhance growth potential. It is evident from the country studies that there are significant gaps between the alignment of structural reform plans in G20 economies and the strategic priorities for growth set by the Organization for Economic Cooperation and Development (OECD). The assessment of members' macroeconomic frameworks also points to low potential growth in advanced surplus economies, highlighting the need for structural reform. Finally, the country studies indicate that reducing imbalances will necessitate structural reforms to also boost potential growth in major advanced economies.

Third, reform policies are needed to remove key distortions and narrow problem imbalances in emerging surplus economies. Limited progress has been made to date on rebalancing global demand and reducing external imbalances. The country studies indicate that policies aimed at reducing the distortions underpinning high national saving in China—including large gaps in the social safety net, financial restrictions, and undervalued exchange rates—will be needed to reduce imbalances, rebalance global demand, and anchor G20 growth objectives.

Upside Scenario

These three policy layers underpin a potential upside scenario. Policies are tailored for the G20 economies to reflect individual country circumstances. These are derived both from the case studies, as well as from IMF staff analysis in the context of the IMF's regular surveillance activities.

Fiscal rebalancing is already advancing, but more will be needed in some deficit G20 members—preferably through "growth-friendly" measures including tax and entitlement reform.[3] As highlighted in the country studies, budgetary consolidation is generally under way (i.e., part of the baseline), but members' efforts will need to be sustained over time. According to policies assumed in IMF staff baseline projections, some members will also need to undertake more fiscal adjustment to meet their commitments, reestablish needed policy space, and ensure sustainable public finances in an upside scenario.[4] In terms of timing, given the still-fragile nature of the recovery, some G20 members will also need to strike the right balance between supporting growth in the near term and more decisive action to consolidate growth over the medium term, especially if economies weaken further. Thus, where added fiscal effort is required, the upside considers the timing of adjustment that depends on country circumstances. Finally, budgetary actions that mitigate the dampening effects on short-run growth and further support external rebalancing and medium-term growth are preferable to help secure members' shared objectives. Toward this end, several specific steps need to be taken in several areas, as outlined below.

---

[3]See Box 10.1 for a more detailed description of the policy and technical assumptions underpinning the upside scenario using the IMF's Global Integrated Monetary and Fiscal (GIMF) model.
[4]For the upside scenario analysis, IMF staff estimates based on members' budgetary plans envisage the need for an additional 1¼ percent of GDP reduction in the overall G20 fiscal deficit in 2016 (and a 3 percent cumulative reduction in fiscal deficits over the medium term, 2012–16).

- *Tax and entitlement reform are critical elements to underpin credible consolidation of sufficient scale.* More credible adjustment, in turn, helps better anchor private sector expectations to advance gains over the medium term. Where possible, a shift toward greater reliance on indirect taxes (e.g., a value-added tax) rather than direct taxes on factor inputs would help limit tax distortions and improve incentives to save and invest. This could be budget-neutral (e.g., in Germany and France) or part of consolidation (e.g., the United States). This could help further reduce external imbalances, depending on the composition quality of fiscal adjustment, while better supporting growth over the medium term. Entitlement reform is a necessary ingredient of any credible fiscal consolidation plan in several G20 members given underfunded obligations and aging of the population. This includes added pension reform to advance the move toward actuarial balance (e.g., France).

- *Private sector rebalancing is at risk of stalling, and more targeted structural reform in key areas should be considered to support potential growth.* To tackle still-high unemployment and weak private sector spending in some advanced G20 members, active labor market policies could be considered to facilitate reallocation and reemployment of displaced workers. Other demand-friendly policies—such as policies to encourage investment—could also be considered in some members. However, it will be important that the rebound in private saving in key deficit economies be maintained and that underlying distortions in the financial sector that gave rise to stability risks be effectively addressed. Over the medium term, structural factors behind low growth potential could be addressed more effectively as highlighted in the country studies. Besides reducing implementation risk, baseline structural reform policies could be strengthened through some reorientation toward problem areas. Specifically, more labor and product market reform in strategic priority areas would enhance growth potential. Based on OECD recommendations, lagging productivity in insular or restricted service sectors could be boosted in several G20 countries (e.g., Japan, France, Germany, China, and India) through competition policies to limit distortions and regulatory reform toward best practices. Product market reforms are also envisaged in other G20 economies (e.g., Australia, Canada, Indonesia, Italy, Korea, Mexico, Russia, and South Africa). On the labor market side, lowering hiring costs (e.g., France, India, Italy, Japan, Korea, and Turkey) and reforming disability insurance benefits (United Kingdom) would strengthen employment prospects. Measures to strengthen female participation rates in Japan and Germany could also support their medium-term growth.

- *Financial sector repair and reform are crucial to sustain the recovery.* Against a backdrop of heightened financial stability risks, it is crucial that decisive near-term action be pursued to resolve the sovereign debt crisis in Europe. Moreover, many advanced economies appear to be mired in the repair-and-recovery phase of the credit cycle with incomplete balance sheet repair. More progress is needed to reduce sovereign spillovers and break the adverse feedback loop between the financial sector and real economy that could jeopardize the recovery. From a modeling perspective, technical limitations prevent an in-depth macroeconomic analysis of financial sector repair and reform in the upside scenario. Nonetheless, from an economic perspective, such policy measures are essential for securing the shared growth objectives and as part of a G20 action plan. Further action to reduce near-term financial sector risks would lay the critical foundations for the strengthened medium-term economic prospects examined in the upside scenario.

BOX 10.1

Policy Assumptions for the G20 Upside Scenario

The upside scenario described in this chapter consists of three layers: (1) additional fiscal consolidation and budget-neutral tax reform; (2) structural reforms in labor and product markets (productivity effects are based on simulation results from the Organization for Economic Cooperation and Development), but have been scaled to take account of G20 members' policies in IMF staff's baseline projections); and (3) rebalancing reforms in China.

G20 members are assumed to fully implement country-specific policies that are identified by the country case studies and the IMF's G20 Mutual Assessment Process reports. In particular, it is assumed that members will undertake the following:

- *Additional fiscal consolidation (relative to currently identified plans).* A cumulative reduction of headline deficit by 2016 is assumed for Japan (3.75 percent of GDP), the United States (2.8 percent), the United Kingdom (2 percent), France (1.1 percent), India (2.3 percent), and other European Union countries (1 percent). The share of instruments used to achieve the consolidation is as follows: for Japan (0.2 percent transfers, 0.8 percent value-added tax [VAT]); the United States (0.25 percent government consumption, 0.5 percent transfers, 0.25 percent VAT); the United Kingdom (0.5 percent government consumption, 0.5 percent transfers); France (0.65 percent government consumption; 0.35 percent VAT); India (0.5 percent government consumption, 0.5 percent VAT); and other European Union countries (0.3 percent government consumption, 0.2 percent VAT, 0.5 percent transfers). Fiscal actions are assumed to be permanent in the year in which they occur.
- *Tax reform.* A revenue-neutral tax reform is simulated for Germany and as part of consolidation for the United States. For Germany and the United States, the increase in indirect taxes (2 and 1.35 percentage points of GDP, respectively) is used to finance equal reductions in personal and corporate income taxes. For France, the higher revenue from indirect taxes (1.5 percentage points) is split 2 to 1 in favor of lowering labor income taxes (mainly social security contributions) versus corporate income taxes. For all three countries, the tax reform lowers distortions by shifting from direct to indirect taxes.
- *Structural reforms.* Two types of structural reforms are considered—product market and labor market reforms. Which of the reforms applies to which countries is

described in more detail below. Reforms that change the participation rate are assumed to be fully credible, while the credibility of those that raise the level of productivity is assumed to grow over time, becoming fully credible after five years. To mitigate deflation risk, reforms to enhance supply potential are phased in gradually and, where possible, "demand friendly" actions in labor markets (e.g., active labor market policies) are also considered in the near term. For the seven G20 countries selected for sustainability analysis in this volume, *product market* reforms are simulated for Japan, France, Germany, China, and India to boost productivity in the nontradable sector. In line with OECD recommendations, the product market reforms comprise an improvement of product market regulation toward best practices. *Labor market reforms* in the form of lower hiring costs are included for Japan, France, and India. In the United States, active labor market policies are considered to help reduce the high long-term unemployment rate, while in the United Kingdom, a reduction in the average replacement rate of disability benefits is assumed. Furthermore, in Japan and Germany, measures to increase female participation rates are considered, while for France, additional reform toward actuarially neutral pension is assumed. For the rest of the G20 membership, the simulations include product market reforms for Australia, Canada, Indonesia, Italy, Korea, Mexico, Russia, and South Africa; labor market reforms (lowering hiring costs) for Italy, Korea, and Turkey; active labor market policies in Brazil; lower average replacement rate of disability benefits in Canada; and pension reform in Turkey.

- *Reform in China.* Finally, the upside scenario assumes reform in China to facilitate global rebalancing. With exchange rate flexibility, the following are considered:

  ➢ *Reform in education and safety nets.* These reforms raise public consumption expenditure by 4 percent of GDP after 10 years and reduce private saving by 10 percent of GDP after 10 years.

  ➢ *Financial sector reform.* These reforms raise the cost of capital to tradable sector firms by 100 basis points after five years and reduce the proportion of liquidity-constrained households by 5 percentage points after five years (10 percentage points after 10 years).

  ➢ *Nontradable sector reforms.* These reforms encourage growth in the nontradable sector that raises both output and demand. The level of service sector productivity increases by 4 percent after 10 years, with the demand for services increasing sufficiently to prevent any exchange rate depreciation.

For the purposes of the upside scenario, further rebalancing policy efforts are also considered only in the systemic case of China based on its sustainability assessment, but they are relevant for other emerging surplus economies.[5] Specifically, education reform and strengthened safety nets (through higher public expenditure) could help reduce high precautionary saving in China. Financial sector

---

[5]An update of the IMF staff's upside scenario—based on policy inputs for all G20 members—can be found in the 2012 Staff Reports for the G20 Mutual Assessment Process. See www.imf.org/external/np/g20/map2012.htm.

reform could help reduce distortions for firms and grant greater access to credit for liquidity-constrained households. This could help boost consumption and reduce inefficient investment. Finally, allowing greater market determination of the exchange rate and accepting greater currency appreciation would reinforce demand rebalancing at higher employment levels and facilitate the reallocation of resources across tradable to nontradable sectors.

Simulated Gains

An upside scenario that brings together all the central policy ingredients demonstrates the collective benefits through higher growth and lower imbalances. The effects of upside policies are shown with respect to (i.e., as deviations from) the IMF's *World Economic Outlook* (WEO) baseline projections (Figure 10.2).[6] The main findings associated with the collection of upside policies are described below.

Additional fiscal consolidation alone would be inimical to global growth at first (Figure 10.3). While critical for restoring soundness to public finances over time, further fiscal consolidation (beyond IMF staff's baseline adjustment) in the major advanced economies will, in isolation, result in a decrease of world GDP by around ½ percent relative to the baseline at the time this withdrawal takes place. More front-loaded consolidation would further risk advancing and deepening these dampening effects on growth (especially given present constraints on monetary policy near the zero interest rate floor). Moreover, fiscal consolidation by itself would carry negative spillovers for partner countries. This underscores the need for well-timed fiscal plans to be as growth friendly as possible in G20 members requiring fiscal adjustment, as well as the need for supportive action by others to offset weaker demand in partner countries.

Specifically, a complementary package of policy actions is required. If the necessary fiscal adjustment is combined with supporting policy measures, the picture progressively changes (Figure 10.4). First, consolidation when combined with budget-neutral tax reform—shifting the composition of revenue instruments away from distortionary taxes—produces adjustment that is more growth friendly. Also in this second layer, better-targeted structural reform in product and labor markets to boost potential growth would add to the growth benefits.[7] Finally, rebalancing policies to reduce domestic distortions and boost internal demand in emerging surplus economies (i.e., China in the simulations) would further lift growth to help offset weaker domestic demand in partners.

Taken together, a cooperative policy action plan has appreciable upside potential for growth. The simulation results show that joint actions by the G20 members consistent with all three policy layers described above, if fully implemented,

---

[6]The simulations are based on the October 2011 WEO projections as the economic and policy baseline, available at the time of the analysis.

[7]Work on the upside scenario analysis for this study was undertaken in close partnership with the OECD. The OECD contributed simulations of the effects of stylized and country-specific structural reforms for individual G20 members based on its past work and expertise.

Figure 10.2 G20 Upside Scenario *(Percent deviation from baseline)*

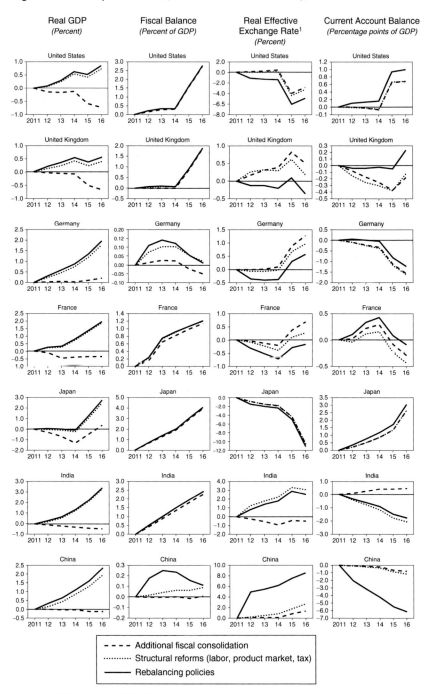

Sources: G20 authorities; and IMF staff estimates.
[1] Increase indicates appreciation.

Figure 10.3 Additional Fiscal Consolidation under the G20 Mutual Assessment Process Upside Scenario *(World real GDP; percent deviation from baseline)*

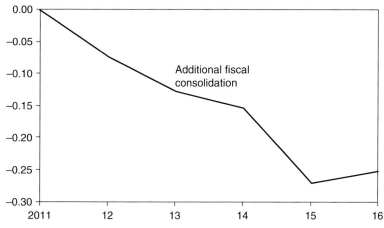

Additional fiscal consolidation

Sources: G20 authorities; and IMF staff estimates.

Figure 10.4 Additional Fiscal Consolidation, Structural Reforms, and Rebalancing Policies under the G20 Mutual Assessment Process Upside Scenario *(World real GDP; percent deviation from baseline)*

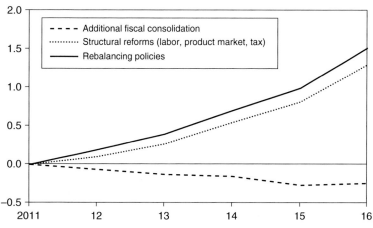

- - - Additional fiscal consolidation
.... Structural reforms (labor, product market, tax)
—— Rebalancing policies

Sources: G20 authorities; and IMF staff estimates.

will result in an overall increase of world GDP by 1½ percent in 2016. This is equivalent to a global income gain of more than $750 billion. This sizable increase in income would add between 20 and 40 million new jobs. In cumulative terms, the upside gains will amount to nearly 3 percent higher global GDP over the medium term. Improved growth prospects across the G20 will be accompanied by significantly lower global imbalances. The simulation results suggest an appreciable reduction of global imbalances by about 3/4 percent of world GDP

Figure 10.5 Current Account Balances *(Percent of world GDP)*

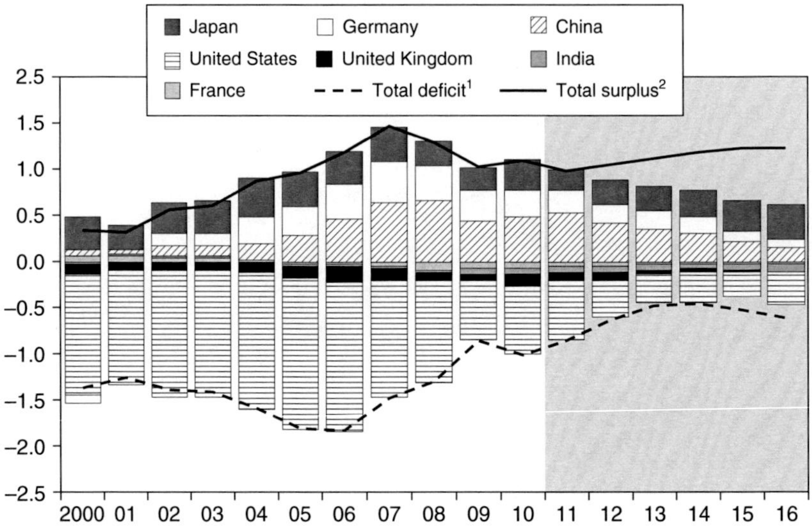

Source: IMF staff estimates.

Note: The period from 2000–10 is from the IMF's World Economic Outlook (WEO) database; the period from 2011–16 reflects WEO projections plus the upside scenario rebalancing shock, except for total deficit and total surplus, which reflect the WEO baseline.

[1]Total for deficit countries in the case studies.
[2]Total for surplus countries in the case studies.

relative to the IMF staff's baseline in 2016 (Figure 10.5). Overall, this improvement is driven by narrowing external imbalances in both deficit and surplus countries.

CONCLUSIONS

In the aftermath of the global financial crisis and the Great Recession, the world economy is still struggling to regain its footing. While the imbalances or "fault lines" associated with the crisis have moderated somewhat, they remain significant enough to warrant serious attention from policymakers around the world. Activity in the advanced economies remains sluggish, partly reflecting the scars left behind by the crisis. In Europe, in particular, the crisis is far from over due in part to large imbalances in the periphery and core and the need to rebuild a more resilient and vibrant monetary union. Meanwhile, in the absence of strong and concerted policy action in other major advanced economies—be it to address fiscal risks or undertake much-needed structural reforms—elevated vulnerabilities pose significant downside risks to growth, prompting worries that another deep downturn is in the offing. Emerging market economies have fared relatively better, but they are not immune to slower growth and risks on this front are increasing. This leaves us with an overall configuration of a slow and bumpy global recovery weighed down by low confidence and prone to setbacks.

Is there a solution to promote stronger, sustainable, and more balanced growth at the global level? This volume has argued that the answer is clearly yes—policymakers working collaboratively can collectively pursue actions to strengthen growth while reducing large imbalances. The challenge is essentially multilateral in nature and involves two rebalancing acts. The first is internal rebalancing. If growth is to be sustained, the countries hardest hit by the crisis need to rebalance away from public support and stimulus toward private demand. The second act is external rebalancing. If growth is to be more balanced, stronger reliance on external demand in major deficit economies needs to be matched by stronger reliance on internal demand in major surplus economies. More symmetric adjustment across deficit and surplus countries would support stronger growth. This would also help avoid a return to a configuration with large macrofinancial imbalances and their attendant risks that existed before the crisis.

Moreover, as shown by the case studies here, tackling many of these key imbalances is not only good for the global economy but also compatible with national interests. Much of the explanation for large imbalances in systemic members of the G20 originates in domestic factors, including distortions and structural issues, underpinning key differences in national saving—too low in major deficit economies and too high in major surplus economies. Efforts to address these underlying distortions or structural impediments can thus boost domestic welfare. Some actions—notably, necessary fiscal consolidation in deficit economies—will strengthen growth prospects only over time and may dampen activity in the near term. Complementary action in surplus economies, however, can make this adjustment less painful while supporting domestic growth in the process. Taken together, collective policy action among the G20 membership can thus provide the foundation for healthier global growth.

As a vehicle for raising awareness of prescient issues, bridging national interests to achieve a common goal, and building consensus aimed at policy coordination, the G20 Mutual Assessment Process (MAP) has a unique opportunity to galvanize such action. It has so far played a useful role in some of these areas, importantly in building a shared understanding of imbalances—including factors underlying them—that need to be addressed expeditiously. It has, however, failed to build consensus on the policy measures needed to reduce imbalances. In addition, the lack of a formal enforcement mechanism or stronger peer review in the process has limited the MAP's traction with policymakers across the G20. Going forward, these shortcomings will need to be addressed if the MAP is to succeed in securing the growth objectives agreed upon by G20 leaders.

Index

[Page numbers followed by *b, f, n,* or *t* refer to boxed text, figures, footnotes, or tables, respectively.]

H

Health care spending
    fiscal imbalances in the United States
        and, 23b, 27
    in France, 69
    in India, 89
    life expectancy in the United States and,
        27f
    recommendations for China, 106
    strategies for improving U.S. economy,
        34
    in the United Kingdom, 41
Housing bubble
    U.K., 39, 43–45, 47–48, 148
    U.S., 7n, 24, 25, 28, 29, 30

I

Incomes, household
    in China, 93–94, 95f, 105
    French household saving and, 76
    in India, 84, 84f
    in Japan, 133, 134
    in U.K., 42, 43f, 44, 46
    U.S. household saving and, 36
India
    balance of payments crisis (1991), 73
    bond market, 89
    causes of imbalances in, 73, 77–85,
        148
    credit access in, 85, 86
    demographic trends in, 85
    financial controls in, 81–84, 89, 90
    Fiscal Responsibility and Budget
        Management Act, 74–75
    future challenges for, 77
    government securities, 81, 83, 83t, 84n
    health care spending, 89
    infrastructure investment, 86
    labor market, 154b
    macroeconomic stability, 87
    private saving and investment in, 73,
        75–77, 76f, 82f, 83f, 84–85
    public debt, 73, 73f, 74–75, 77, 86–87

public saving and investment in, 75,
    76f
public spending in, 78–79, 88–89
recent economic performance, 73–77,
    74f
revenue collection, 78, 79–81, 87–88,
    90
significance of fiscal imbalances in,
    85–87
size of deficits, 73
social indicators, 78, 78t, 79
strategies for addressing imbalances in,
    87–90
subsidy programs, 88
sustainability assessment, 5–6b
Indicative guidelines for sustainability
    assessments, 4–6, 5–6b, 5f
Interest rates
    in China, 100, 101, 104, 104f
    future prospects for the United States,
        31, 33
    global financial crisis and, 29n
    global spillovers of rebalancing in
        China, 107
    India's, 81–82, 83–84
    model of cross-border effects, 16–18
    saving behavior and, 47
    as source of global imbalances, 13–14
    in the United Kingdom, 47, 50
    in the United States, 24, 25, 29, 31, 33
Internal imbalances
    causes of, in France, 60–61
    causes of, in India, 73, 77–85
    causes of, in the United States, 22, 23,
        23b, 26–28
    development in India, 73, 74–75
    development in the United States, 21,
        22f, 25
    future challenges for the United States,
        27–28
    future prospects for France, 59–60
    in Germany, 118
    outcomes of global financial crisis in the
        United States, 27
    patterns in France, 58–59